Living the Vision

LIVING THE VISION

Religious Vows in an Age of Change

Barbara Fiand

CROSSROAD • NEW YORK

1990

The Crossroad Publishing Company
370 Lexington Avenue, New York, N. Y. 10017

Printed in the United States of America

Library of Congress Cataloging-in Publication Data

Fiand, Barbara.
    Living the vision : religious vows in an age of change / Barbara
Fiand.
        p.   cm.
    ISBN 0–8245–1019–4
    1. Vows. I. Title.
BX2435.F48   1990
248.8′94—dc20   89–49182
                                                            CIP

To
Clare Gebhardt and Catherine Griffiths,
companions on the journey,
in friendship and gratitude.

Contents

Preface

It is said that Sigmund Freud once tipped his hat to himself when passing a large wall mirror, only to recognize with embarrassment that the one he had greeted was not a stranger but himself. A similar experience was mine not long ago when I was giving a workshop in a stately old mansion whose former owners had generously endowed it with mirrors in every conceivable spot. I was forever peeking in on myself, intruding on my own privacy.

It is a strange quirk of human self-awareness that has us perceive ourselves without instant recognition; see ourselves without immediately knowing it. The fact that we are usually embarrassed when this happens might indicate that somehow we are surprised at it; that we really expect to have better self-awareness, a clearer presence to ourselves. Perhaps we begin to suspect that something is not quite harmonized in our perception, in our vision of who we are. Perhaps also this rather extroverted occurrence uncomfortably reminds us of the much more complex matter of inner awareness and depth perception to which all of us are called, in which, however, we are all wanting to varying degrees.

Giving this latter insight serious consideration is a painful business, one we would probably all rather avoid. Why is it that we "have eyes but do not see"—at least not as we might? Could one of the reasons perhaps be that so many of us are spending too much of our time and energy reacting and responding to the periphery of reality, be it internal or external, and thus, often unknowingly and with the best intentions, are losing sight of what really counts? The mystic warns us that "God is the circle's center for those who dare embrace Him [Her]. For those

1

who merely stand in awe, [S/he] is the circle's rim."* Are we perhaps so much in awe that we forget to plunge into the center?

The title of this book evolved over a number of years that for me, as for most of us in religious life, were spent rewriting constitutions, reformulating government plans, community policies; in other words, *looking at ourselves*. Like others during these years, I kept wondering about the meaning of it all even as I was engaged in the process. I saw us expend a great deal of energy as we met, planned, and debated for hours. I saw the documents that resulted. They were read and then neatly put away on our shelves or in our drawers as we went about discussing, debating, and rewriting further documents. I found the experience interesting; useful for good organization and management. I kept wondering, however, whether, in *looking* at ourselves, we were really *seeing*; whether, in expecting the questions we were asking about ourselves to be answered, we were really *questioning*; whether we were in awe of the rim of our lives together and were loosing our yearning for deeper vision, our quest for the center. Somehow in our discussions together I kept hearing questions that no one (including myself) was asking aloud; I kept sensing concerns about issues that we were not raising; I kept experiencing a hunger that none of our meetings and documents could satisfy, and I kept feeling that I was not alone in this. And so I decided to write and to probe into the meaning of *vision*.

Writing, at times, is easier than speaking, especially for an introvert. One moves into the quiet of one's self and there lets everything that one has heard and seen play around, dance in the heart of one's very being until a focus is reached and insight breaks through. The pain but also the excitement of writing is in the waiting; in letting the dance be dance, the play be play; in not forcing the process. This kind of writing is the exact opposite of Robert's Rules of Order to which so many of our discussions, planning sessions, assemblies, and chapters are still, even today, being subjected. Hence, this kind of writing is freeing. It lets the question be and does not worry about "absolute" or "simple" majority. As a consequence, of course, it cannot pro-

*Frederick Franck, *Messenger of the Heart* (New York: Crossroad, 1976), p. 53.

vide many "guidelines," many final solutions, fixed answers. It rather lets questions move into deeper questions and recognizes the light in what appears to be darkness. It honors the process of emergence. The vision that bears witness to this emergence is much like a child's experience of sunrise. It is filled with wonder, with prayer.

I do not know how often, in the writing of these pages, something entirely different from what I had planned came to word. Perhaps a similar experience will grace the reader. What you expect to find (and perhaps even what I would like you to find in these pages) may not be here. My prayer is that you can allow this and thus move into the openness of deeper possibilities; of finding in these reflections what presents itself to *you*; of being with *that* and of someday, as the right moment emerges, sharing *that* with your congregation.

It is my hope that this book will be meaningful to religious of every age group; to men and women alike. These pages do, however, have some areas of difficulty and they, for most readers, will probably be found right at the beginning. Because all modes of conscious life are influenced by the culture in which they flourish, I began this book with a reflection on the "age of change" in which we live our vows. Ours is a time when cultural paradigms are collapsing and the dualistic worldview that served so well for centuries in bringing us not only progress and prosperity but also the spirituality to support them, has reached the limits of its own possibilities and is beckoning us from within its own demise to move beyond it and look for deeper, more authentic ways of seeing. An explanation of dualism, of its origin and influence, and of the spirituality it engendered can make for somewhat difficult reading. I wish, therefore, I could invite the reader simply to avoid these preliminary observations and look for greener pastures in the later part of chapter 1, where holistic spirituality is discussed. The issue, however, is not as simple as that. Holistic spirituality as the basis for living our vows in contemporary times can be appreciated only when viewed in relation to the dualism in which most of us were reared. The comparison between holistic and dualistic spirituality, their origin and message is, therefore, of the essence in laying a meaningful foundation for the rest of the book.

Chapter 2 attempts to demonstrate this by exploring the implications of a holistic perspective for the self-understanding of men and women religious. It concentrates specifically on issues of ministry, of membership and governance, and explores how our vision changes when we approach each other as a "society of equals," as members of Christ's *basileia*. It stresses the primacy of disposition in living the vows and moves us, I hope, away from seeking a foolproof ground plan or guide. Its intent is to open up the deeper realities that entice us from the "rim" to the "center" of our lives, from power and control to surrender.

The next three chapters concern themselves with our vows in the order in which we usually profess them: poverty, consecrated celibacy, and obedience. In each case I have attempted to explore the vow first within the context of the holistic paradigm developed in chapters 1 and 2. This, then, is followed by some reflections on the practical concerns that address us in the existential situations of everyday life. What is presented here is intended to be open ended. I make no pretensions of having the final word on any of the issues raised. That, quite clearly, would betray the main objective of these reflections, namely, to identify consecrated life in particular, and the dedicated life of the believer generally, as a spiraling process of ever-expanding vision, of an ever-deepening movement into God. No one in this process stands as a solitary prophet or primary wisdom figure. As community, our insights must be shared and challenged toward the deeper vision of the whole. The questions at the end of all chapters are designed to further this. Their intention is at all times to expand the reflective process begun through the reading of the chapter and to enhance the involvement of the reader in the vision itself.

The book ends with some thoughts on membership. I owe these in large measure to the wonderful women and men from diverse religious congregations who participated in the Studies of Spirituality Program of the Archdiocese of Cincinnati. I met them in the first years of their discernment and learned much from them. I learned of their hopes and dreams, their willingness to serve, their dedication. I learned to love them, trust them, and respect them. They gave me hope for the future of religious life, but their insights and observations also left me with some concerns. Chapter 6 speaks to both.

This book is clearly concerned with the consecrated life of religious. It is, however, not written exclusively for them. The body that is Christ has many members and, as Paul tells us (1 Cor. 12:12–27), each member needs the other. The secluded life of religious in the past may have given the impression to their Christian brothers and sisters that they lived their relationship to God apart from the rest of the Christian community. This, if it ever has been true, can be true no longer. Just as religious in the past several years have become actively involved in ministry with married couples and, therefore, had to learn about consecrated matrimony, so, it seems to me, married and single persons also need to support, minister to, and know their brothers and sisters in religious life. Our call is to serve God in diverse ways according to our gifts; always, however, for the unity of the body. For this, interdependence and support are essential. The glory and the brokenness of religious life are offered in these pages, therefore, for the prayer of the membership. "If one member suffers, all the members suffer with it; if one member is honored, all the members share its joy" (1 Cor. 12:26).

There are many whom I wish to thank for their help and encouragement in writing this book. My gratitude goes first and foremost to my own congregation for encouraging the dance within my heart, the play within my thoughts, to come to expression in the S.N.D. position paper on the vowed life I wrote a few years back. Thanks also to my sisters in Ipswich, Massachusetts, for inviting my first lectures on this topic and, after them, to the many religious congregations throughout the country who kept the issues burning within me. A special thank you to the Sisters of Mercy of Cincinnati who allowed the taping of my reflections on the vows for St. Anthony Messenger Press (*Living Religious Vows in an Age of Change—A Holistic Approach*; four cassette tapes). My gratitude, once again, to the publisher, editors, and staff of The Crossroad Publishing Company, especially to Michael Leach, Frank Oveis, and Eugene Gollogly, for their graciousness and their support. To the numerous friends with whom I have shared and reflected, to my students who encouraged my writing, and to the Athenaeum of Ohio for time to think and write, my heartfelt thanks. Finally, in a very special way, I wish to thank those women and men who believe in the call to witness to consecration and mission through community life. I want to thank you for your faith, for your hope, and for your perseverance.

1

Turning Point

[In the Chinese province of Kiaochau] there was a great drought. For months there had not been a drop of rain and the situation became catastrophic. The Catholics made processions, the Protestants made prayers and the Chinese burned joss-sticks and shot off guns to frighten away the demons of the drought, but with no result. Finally the Chinese said, "We will fetch the rainmaker." And from another province a dried-up old man appeared. The only thing he asked for was a quiet little house somewhere, and there he locked himself in for three days. On the fourth day the clouds gathered and there was a great snow storm at the time of the year when no snow was expected, an unusual amount, and the town was so full of rumors about the wonderful rainmaker that Richard Wilhelm went to ask the man how he did it. In true European fashion he said, "They call you the rainmaker, will you tell me how you made the snow?" And the little Chineseman said, "I did not make the snow, I am not responsible." "But what have you done these three days?" "Oh, I can explain that. I come from another country where things are in order. Here they are out of order, they are not as they should be by the ordinance of heaven. Therefore the whole country is not in Tao, and I also am not in the natural order of things because I am in a disordered country. So I had to wait three days until I was back in Tao and then naturally the rain came.[1]

This story, discussed by Jungian analyst Jean Shinoda Bolen in her book *The Tao of Psychology*, speaks symbolically to what she calls a "drought mentality," of the psyche. It signifies a state of dis-ease and anxiety caused by a lack of inner order, a feeling of being severed from the Whole (the Tao). The orientation of this anxiety, claims Bolen, points almost exclusively toward the fu-

ture, filling the psyche with the dread of insufficiency and being
self-fulfilling in its inordinance. To return to wholeness and re-
store fertility and creativity (rain) requires becoming centered
once again—finding one's "quiet little house"—in order to become still, to experience the One.

How might Bolen's story apply to the many concerns and issues that address religious life in contemporary times? My sense
is that we can find great relevance in it, and that the call to return to quiet inner ordering so that we might overcome the
noise and drought, and encounter creativity once more in our
lives and our communities, will become ever more audible once
we allow ourselves to listen to the silence within and orient ourselves toward the One. Nor does the "drought mentality" afflict
only us. Bolen's story points beyond, I believe, to our culture
and to the entire perceptive framework of contemporary Western society. No human phenomenon ever appears in isolation.
We are essentially with-others-in-the-world. Their vision affects
us. What afflicts them, afflicts us and vice versa. The call to
"leave the world and not allow oneself to be 'contaminated' by
it" may sound plausible to Thomas à Kempis, but sociologically
it is a fallacy. Religious, like all other humans, are culturally affected. To understand ourselves, then, we have to understand, at
least in broad strokes, the *what* and *why* of contemporary world
perspectives.

Culture in Crisis

We live in difficult times, times of great change and uncer-
tainty, times of conflict and doubt, of social as well as ethical
confusion. Those "who know"—philosophers, theologians, social and physical scientists alike—tell us that the difficulties we
experience are global, that in every facet of our lives we are
faced with insights and discoveries that can no longer be contained in the concepts and categories with which we were once
comfortable; concepts and categories that for centuries assured
us with clear absolutes and gave us the answers we needed to
preserve the present and contain the future with optimism. Ours
is an age of crisis, calling us toward what Fritjof Capra, the
well-known atomic physicist turned mystic, diagnoses as one

monumental turning point of perception, a gigantic shift in attitude[2]—in the way we have been used to seeing, judging, as well as responding to reality: to ourselves, to the world, and to God.

The turning point that Capra is suggesting is, of course, hardly something easily achieved or even seen as desirable by most of us, caught, as we are, in the millstream of transition. No civilization lets go easily of the perspective through which it has achieved its glory and with which it has grown comfortable. Hence rigidity and inflexibility are often the precursors of ultimate crisis and are a major factor in its agony. Capra, citing Toynbee, explains it well:

After civilizations have reached a peak of vitality, they tend to lose their cultural steam and decline. An essential element in this cultural breakdown . . . is a loss of flexibility. When social structures and behavior patterns have become so rigid that the society can no longer adapt to changing situations, it will be unable to carry on the creative process of cultural evolution. It will break down and, eventually, disintegrate.

The "drought mentality," in other words, has set in and starvation is bound to follow.

Whereas growing civilizations display endless variety and versatility, those in the process of disintegration show uniformity and lack of inventiveness. The loss of flexibility in a disintegrating society is accompanied by a general loss of harmony among its elements, which inevitably leads to the outbreak of social discord and disruption."[3]

One needs little evidence to recognize these phenomena as of our time. Discord and disruption abound everywhere. Psychologists call ours an age of alienation and write volumes about anxiety. National as well as international inflexibilities insist that there is only one way, one's own way, and so billions are spent on "weapons for peace," and mistrust of anyone who speaks of dialogue and of living with differences is widespread—always, of course, "in the interests of national security." Within the church this phenomenon is echoed. Here our inflexibility rises "in defense of the faith," and of the authority of the magisterium. It stifles any and all creative rethinking of "tradition."

Symbolically speaking, it seems that Western civilization needs to withdraw into its "quiet little house" and silence itself into harmony with the universe once again, in order to be able to take hold of the opportunities that light up for it in this crisis. We might note that the Chinese term for crisis *(wei-ji)* speaks of both *danger* and *opportunity*.[4] The philosopher Martin Heidegger, known so well for his depth insight into our contemporary dilemma, speaks in the same vein when he assures us that "where there is danger there deliverance thrives as well."[5] Crisis appears as a dimension of transformation. "We live today in a globally interconnected world, in which biological, psychological, social, and environmental phenomena are all interdependent."[6] To describe this world correctly and begin to understand its dilemma, Capra sees the need for an "ecological perspective," a perspective that I would prefer to call *holistic* in order to distinguish it more clearly and more immediately from the dualistic worldview that, I believe, has brought our society and our culture to this point in history and to this crisis.

Dualism

Dualism, the cornerstone of Western thought for millennia, might in its systematic articulation be traced back as far as Greek idealism and the Greco-Roman worldview, though modern analysts frequently give it a more modest beginning in Descartes, ascribing the mechanistic worldview flowering from it to Newtonian physics. For our purposes its Greco-Roman beginning will have more meaning, for the Greeks and their passionate preoccupation with permanence in the midst of change were responsible for first systematically dividing the world of reality into spirit and matter, soul and body, the sacred and the profane, certainty and illusion, the superior and the inferior, good and evil, the masculine and the feminine—with the former to be sought after; the latter at best to be avoided, at worst to be endured.

Most interpretations of reality spring, I believe, from some form (fair or foul) of self-awareness and consequent self-reflection, with subsequent projection outward. It was so with the primitive's fertility rights and continues to be so, consciously or not, in most contemporary theories, from economics to psychology and even criminology. We are, therefore, not too far afield if we imagine that our Greek ancestors did the same. Looking at themselves and their relation to time and change, they became convinced that much pain and loss (hence evil) accompanies transitoriness, while permanence brings with it stability and trustworthiness (the good). Their own embodiment spoke, of course, of change. It was matter (in later Latin times not only theoretically but, in fact, etymologically linked with woman: *mater*—mother; *materia*—matter). That which held their identity intact even as their body decayed they called "soul"—"spirit." Matter became the principle of change and illusion; spirit became the principle of permanence and truth.

We are all familiar, at least somewhat, with dualistic metaphysics, for it became the hallmark of Western Christendom. From Augustine and Augustinianism through Anselm and medieval scholasticism, it permeated Christian thought to the point of exclusivity and virtual canonization. (Many a mystic was condemned for erring from it.) Ultimately, of course, it led to "Ockham's razor" and to universal skepticism, only to be revived again in Descartes and modern enlightenment. In contemporary times we meet its reverse side in materialism and encounter its results in almost total nihilism: the death of all values, the theater of the absurd.

Dualistic spirituality, which is dominant in our church even to this day, holds within it both the hierarchical as well as the patriarchal view of the sacred. The hierarchical springs naturally from the dualistic, for if half of reality is seen as good and the other as evil, if one half can be trusted and must be sought after and the other must be avoided, it is easy to conceive of an inbuilt perceptive framework where "better than," "higher than," "more noble than," "holier than," are naturally placed in opposition to the other half, and qualities are even divided internally and ranked according to their proximity to spirit and remoteness from matter. The exact origin of patriarchy seems unclear. What is not unclear, however, is its dualistic orientation. As Jungian analyst Edward C. Whitmont points out:

The religious trends which characterized the era of patriarchal ego development were based on the devaluation of natural life and matter, of mundane existence, and of the body. Concrete reality, as we encounter it, was increasingly devoid of the spirit and opposed to it. The inwardness of being in the world, which is the realm of the Feminine, was rejected.

Misogyny [hatred of woman] and androlatry [male sidedness], then, are indissolubly intertwined with the religious convictions and beliefs that were held during the last two to four thousand years or more.[7]

We face today the results of a dualistic, patriarchal, and hierarchical spirituality. It permeates still, even after Vatican II, our liturgies and prayers, our ecclesial structures and mandates, our church's official presence in the world, and many of the structures of religious life. We were all reared in it, trained as religious to see through its set of glasses, judge with its measuring sticks, weigh with its scales. So used to it are we that many of us might balk in disbelief and consternation at the suggestion that there can be another way of interpreting reality; another way of experiencing ourselves and our relation to each other, the world, and God; a way equally valid and profoundly Christian, but holistic rather than dualistic. The reason for this disbelief and dis-ease is that spirituality, as Anne Carr says so well, is "all-encompassing and pervasive. . . . [It] reaches into our unconscious or half-conscious depths. And while it shapes behavior and attitudes, spirituality is more than a conscious code. In relation to God, it is who we really are, the deepest self."[8] We dwell in our spirituality much more than we profess it. It is the ambiance—that which allows us to see, to reflect on, to interpret, and ultimately respond to the depth questions of our existence. It colors our seeing, our hearing, our speaking, even our breathing.[9] Little wonder, then, that questioning the predominant spirituality of an age—the guiding spirituality of an individual—can cause insecurity and upset.

Spirituality is expressed in everything we do. It is a style, unique to the self, that catches up all our attitudes: in communal and personal prayer, in behavior, bodily expressions, life choices, in what we support and affirm and what we protest and deny. . . .

[It] is deeply informed by family, teachers, friends, community, class, race, culture, sex, and by our time in history, just as it is influenced by beliefs, intellectual positions, and moral options.[10]

It is our deepest myth, the energy that supplies our imagination and our feelings, and directs our understanding. Our involvement with it and in it is intense, therefore, although not necessarily always conscious. To feel shaken in it is to experience tremors in the very depths of one's being and these are intensified in direct proportion to one's unconsciousness. Just as our deepest self may be partially hidden from us, even though it energizes our actions and informs our world perspective and our values, so our spirituality can remain quite hidden from conscious awareness and therefore remain unexamined. Larger and deeper than speculative theology, it lacks theological specificity and speaks rather from within the wider cultural, racial, sexual mythos that inspires theological articulation and in turn gets nourished by it. It is the soil, if you will, from which theology sprouts; a soil, however, that, for the sake of theological clarity and specificity, has been tilled and cultivated in our Western tradition, leaving much of its originality unthought.

Thinking into Our Myths

To think into and bring to consciousness our myths means that we can "affirm or deny them, accept parts and reject others, as we grow in relationship to God, to others, to our world."[11] Thinking into our myths has us, therefore, move beyond them even as we stand within them. It frees us to respond in ever-greater depth to their message concerning the ultimate questions of our existence. It empowers us to take their answers and move with them into still deeper questions about our origin and our end: where we came from and why, who we are and how we should live, where our home is and how we might return there. Thinking into our myths in contemporary society means, however, more so now than ever before, doing this also within the context of other disciplines: of archeology and anthropology, of psychology, sociology, biology, and physics, of linguistics, philosophy, and history. This is so because thinking into our myths today means facing the crisis of our culture and accepting its mandate toward transformation. This requires honesty, integrity, and courage. We can no longer be satisfied with religious isolationism or authoritarian absolutism precisely because both of these originate within the very culture and myth that is in crisis and needs to be transformed. To think into our myths, therefore, requires an openness to the possibility of a radical regrounding of our spirituality, a "revolution of consciousness," as Beatrice Bruteau calls it, where we take the risk and allow for a genuine "gestalt shift in the whole way of seeing our relations to one another so that our behavior patterns are reformed from the inside out."[12] This is no easy task. It asks for a courageous facing of what will no longer do, and a rethinking of everything that perpetuates dualism in its divisiveness, elitism, isolationism, and exclusivity. It means bringing to the surface, to conscious reflection, the fundamental questions that undergird all spirituality and which for most of us have remained, with their roots generally unthought and unquestioned, within the realm of blind faith:

—Who is our God?
—Who are we?
—How are we related to our God—in authenticity and righteousness, or in alienation and sin?
—How can we return home? What is redemption?

Thinking into our myths means probing the answers to these questions in their effects on our values and our behavior. It means regrounding them within the ecological and holistic perspective that may help us through the crisis of our times back into harmony with the One.

We all know the God of dualism. At the risk of appearing simplistic, one might present the following synopsis:* The God of dualism is a patriarchal ruler, different from a parent in his wrath and remoteness (though called Father), exacting love, holding obedience as primary. He (and there is no doubt about his gender) made the world out of nothing in six days and on the seventh day he rested, obliging all of us (under pain of sin) to do the same in imitation and worship of him. The God of dualism is a "mighty fortress," a "bulwark," Lord of lords,

*It is important to note that in presenting this I am not primarily concerned with strict orthodoxy. My interest lies rather with the mythos and its sphere of influence: how it infiltrates our broad self-understanding vis-à-vis the Holy and our overall value orientation and behavior.

King of kings. Only consecrated ministers (men) can approach his sanctuary, and consecrated fingers touch him. His love for us is an issue of faith. He sends suffering as chastisement, for "our own good," and because he loves us. When good things happen to us we are grateful to him, though we also look anxiously toward tomorrow because these moments are usually "too good to be true." Paradoxically, we can also reject this God (lose our faith) for his interference in our lives, since "an all-good God would never allow us to suffer so much."

A dualistic interpretation of reality also clearly identifies *our* place in the scheme of things. Ours is a divided humanity: man was made in God's image; Eve, his helpmate, was a secondary creature. Thomas saw her as an "incomplete male"; Augustine wondered whether she had a soul.[13] Humans, from the first sin onward, have been depraved. We are originally sinful. Our relation to God was cut off. We inherited our depravity through the intercourse of our parents. (This view is consistent with a general rejection of the body and of human sexuality.) Our body is viewed as distinct from our soul (its prison, in fact) while it sojourns in "this valley of tears." The primary sin was disobedience and pride—a desire to be like God. The contrasting virtues, therefore, are obedience (preferably blind and quick) and humility, seen as self-debasement and abnegation, and judged frequently through external acts symbolizing this. As religious we remember well our "acts of humility" and self-abnegation, as well as our overall "punishment" of the body.

Redemption, in a dualistic-patriarchal system, is achieved through restitution, through suffering in order to "pay the price for sin." It is an "opening of the gates of heaven" through retribution offered to an offended deity—retribution that, because of the enormity of the sin against God himself, had to be paid for by God also. Only God can appease God. Dying for our sins was willed by God and submitted to by Christ in perfect obedience to the Father as a peace offering restoring us to grace. Through Christ's death we became a "holy people," unworthy though we are.

The paradigm fleshed out here may appear rough and, for the sophisticated reader trained in post–Vatican II theology, it may even be somewhat offensive. What needs to be remembered here is that refinements in theology have little effect on the average believer if the foundational myth remains unthought and un-questioned. Thus, for example, it may be true that today few of us remain concerned about mortal sin associated with Sunday work and we may even be familiar with an up-to-date exegesis of the creation story and have studied contemporary theology concerning sin, yet who of us has really replaced the previous preoccupation with sin with an understanding of the meaning of creative celebration, of work as cosmic liberation, and of rest as joy-filled contemplation of goodness and harmony?

One might dismiss this sort of challenge as impossible in our times and in our culture. Ours is the age of workaholism. If we are not at our jobs, we work at relaxing and worry when we have nothing to do. That, of course, is precisely the point. The roots of workaholism are the same as obligatory rest on the Sab-bath. Neither flow from obedience to one's own integrity and one's creative unity with the cosmos; from listening there to the goodness that calls us into a celebration with all of creation. Both of them, rather, are *externally induced* and are effective be-cause of a fundamental distrust of self. The one obliges under pain of sin, exacting worship—the official surrender of time to the *spiritual* over against the *material* concerns of life. The other springs from the need to "make it" in a world where material gain identifies one's status, one's worthiness, and spirit has been dismissed as irrelevant. That the coercion in either case comes from different sources—one from religion, the other from the broader society and culture; one from *spiritualism*, the other from *materialism*—is irrelevant. Both are grounded in a split world-view that needs reconciliation

The "acts of humility" cited above are another case in point. If self-abnegation and the general rejection of the body is no longer an issue today, the self-aggrandizement and the craving for suc-cess, prestige, and recognition so prevalent in its stead (and reli-gious are not immune to this), is merely its other side. What underlies both is a profound sense of personal insignificance and a need to acquiesce to external norms.

As a final example to illustrate that what we are concerned with here is foundational rather than merely speculative, we might briefly turn to a consideration of the issue concerning

God's gender. Experience seems to confirm over and over that explanations and argumentation about the theological incorrectness of attributing gender to God have little effect on removing the masculinized orientation of ecclesial regulations and language still operative today. They often merely upset men and women alike, since they profoundly disturb the mythos. "Woman power" does not appear capable of removing the stigma of sexism in our church either. Frequently it only enhances it, for it is often merely a reaction to it, caught in the same cultural dichotomy that has afflicted our imagination for thousands of years. *Who* has power is, after all, not the point. The power used to *overpower* and exclude is what needs reflection and subsequent healing. The matters we are dealing with here are beyond the intellect alone. They touch us at our very deepest sensitivities. Sandra Schneiders puts it well when she points out:

A healthy spirituality requires a healing of the *imagination* which will allow us not only to think differently about God but to *experience God differently*. The imagination is accessible not primarily to abstract ideas but to language, images, interpersonal experience, symbolism, art—*all the integrated approaches which appeal simultaneously to intellect, will, and feeling.*[14]

Refounding Our Myths

We have found ourselves for years now, both culturally and ecclesially, trying to straighten things out in isolation from each other and piecemeal, somewhat like the Catholics, the Protestants, and the Chinese in Kiaochau before they joined together and called for the rainmaker. Our answer lies in entering the "quiet little house" and becoming one with each other and all of creation. This clearly calls for a different paradigm than the one we are used to. Our worldview seems to have reached its "limit-situation."

For individual development and maturation, coming to a limit situation means that one has reached that level of growth where the old perceptions and ways of responding will no longer do and new levels of insight are imminent but have not as yet broken through. There is, therefore, for the individual a general sense of confusion and chaos, and even of helplessness, while she or he can do little else but wait for a "new dawn":

In a limit-situation, [one] loses [one's] foothold . . . becomes suddenly aware of the fundamental limitations of [one's] existence, and discovers the radical contingency of all beings encountered. In a limit-situation, [our] familiar world loses its solidity and its obviousness, and begins to disintegrate as the ultimate anchorage of [our] existence. A limit-situation reveals the fundamental limits of any and all particular things and situations. It points within these situations to a possible transcendency, indicating thereby that there is something more fundamental, without revealing what that something more fundamental really is.[15]

The cultural parallel here is easily apparent from this analysis. John Shea, on the cover of his paperback edition of *Stories of God: An Unauthorized Biography*, spells it out for us and takes us even deeper:

When we reach our limits, when our ordered worlds collapse, when we cannot enact our moral ideals, when we are disenchanted, we often enter into the awareness of Mystery. We are inescapably related to this Mystery which is immanent and transcendent, which issues invitations we must respond to, which is ambiguous about its intentions, and which is real and important beyond all else.

Our dwelling within Mystery is both menacing and promising, a relationship of exceeding darkness and undeserved light.[16]

I believe this is our situation today. Our cultural limit-situation is ripe at its very core for a "new dawn," for the revelation and encounter with Mystery. The question, nevertheless, nags: What might we hope for in this "possible transcendency"? What might light up out of this "new openness"?

I do not think that what will grace us, as we gather ourselves in the silence of our "quiet little house" and open ourselves toward reconciliation with all of creation, will be anything *new*, if "new" implies "totally foreign." Heidegger tells us that our future, paradoxically, comes toward us out of our past. And so it is, I believe, with our call from dualism to wholeness. Fundamentally it is a homecoming to that which has always been there at the root of our Christian heritage and is now simply drawing us out of our forgetfulness and lostness into awareness.

Though Greco-Roman dualism has been with us for so long now that we can hardly conceive of anything other, scholars assure us that, despite theology's attraction to it throughout the ages, it was anything but the power behind the Christian inspiration. Jesus was a Jew and his movement was part of the Jewish history of his time. His concern, like the concern of all other Jewish movements prevalent in his day, was with the reign of God (God's *basileia*), and Israel's role as God's holy people. "However, the Jesus movement refused to define the holiness of God's elected people in cultic terms, redefining it instead as the wholeness intended in creation."[17] Inclusive wholeness, not a division between the sacred and the profane, pervades the vision of Jesus who sees the *basileia* of God as already present (realized eschatology), even as our eyes are opened and our hearts are softened to acknowledge it.

The central symbolic actualization of the *basileia* vision of Jesus is not the cultic meal but the festive table of a royal banquet or wedding feast. . . . None of the stories told by or about Jesus evidences the concern for ritual purity and moral holiness so typical of other groups in Greco-Roman Palestine. . . . [H]e does not share their understanding that the "holiness" of the Temple and Torah is the locus of God's power and presence.[18]

God's power was with God's people and was evidenced in Christ's healing mission, his inclusion of the sick, the poor, the broken, prostitutes, tax collectors, men and women alike—a "discipleship of equals," as Elisabeth Schüssler Fiorenza identifies it:

The God of Israel is the creator of all human beings, even the maimed, the unclean, and the sinners. . . . Wholeness spells holiness and holiness manifests itself precisely in human wholeness. Everyday life must not be measured by the sacred holiness of the Temple and Torah, but Temple and Torah praxis must be measured and evaluated by whether or not they are inclusive of every person in Israel and whether they engender the wholeness of every human being. Everydayness, therefore, can become revelatory, and the presence and power of God's sacred wholeness can be experienced in *every* human being.[19]

Edward Schillebeeckx, in his reflection *On Christian Faith*, reiterates Schüssler Fiorenza's position when, citing the church father Irenaeus, he insists that "God's honour lies in the happiness,

liberation and salvation or wholeness of humanity." Our belief in
the creation *means* "that God loves us without conditions or limits: undeservedly on our side, boundlessly."[20] This Christian
trust was grounded in the experience of "Jesus' career: from his
message and his life-style which matched it, from the specific
circumstances of his death, and finally from the apostolic witness of his resurrection from the dead."[21] The early Jesus movement lived in the energy of Christ's vision, standing against
dehumanization and the oppression of the patriarchal culture and
time in which it arose. The *basileia* included everyone. Its concern was the wholeness of all. Jesus' "announcement of 'escha-
tological reversal'—many who are first will be last and those last
will be first . . . applies also to women and to their impairment
by patriarchal structures."[22] His vision, therefore, spelled the
death knell to patriarchy and hierarchy alike. He neither experienced nor addressed God as patriarch. Though the cultural con-
straints placed upon him as teacher and proclaimer of God's plan
for humanity in a particular place and time rendered it necessary
to present God as Father,[23] Jesus, in no way, exemplified a patriarchal relation with his God. In fact the very opposite is true.
A patriarch is not addressed as *Abba*. Jesus completely purified
the Old Testament father-son metaphor of its "patriarchal over-
tones," says Sandra Schneiders. He "drew his God image from
the non-patriarchal presentation of God as the deeply offended
but infinitely forgiving father of Israel."[24]

Time and purpose does not permit me to explore this matter
further. Much has, anyhow, already been written on this topic
with greater expertise. The question that, for our purposes, we
need still to ask ourselves, however, is why this ancient heritage
did not survive.

Schüssler Fiorenza's historical interpretation, which sees the
Christian missionary movement expanding the early Palestine
community and reaching out to, yet at the same time becoming
infiltrated by, the Greco-Roman culture, is perhaps the most
easily understood explanation.[25] No missionary ever remains
unaffected by the society to which she or he proclaims the Good
News. To "go forth and teach all nations" always will mean
also being taught and influenced by them in turn. Social and
psychological pressures, as well as time and constant interaction,

wear on the purity of any vision; thus adaptation seems inevitable. From Paul's catechetical use of the "altar to the unknown god" to Nicea and Chalcedon, Greek metaphysics (not only with simple concepts, but also with its tendency to reduce intellectual [faith] movements to systems and bring unity, clarity, and permanence where there had been diversity and process) moved steadily into the Christian tradition. Often this subtle take-over was enhanced by the church's efforts to meet dissenters from the faith on their own turf. If that turf, as was generally the case, turned out to be metaphysical, a defense of the faith became metaphysical; hence the conflict-resolving dogma that was finally pronounced to the whole church was clothed in metaphysical language as well.

Joseph S. O'Leary explains this intermeshing well. The primary hope of the Greek fathers, he points out, had been to "take captive" Greek intellectuality for the use of Gospel explanation and defense. "But there is perhaps no such thing as a one-way conquest, and it can be said as well that the Gospel of Christ was taken captive by Greek intellectuality."[26] As heresies multiplied, the common use of concepts and terminology increased, since the church, in order to preserve the integrity of the Gospel, became ever more specific in its identification of the elements of the faith. Thus,

As the basic principles of philosophy were increasingly redefined in Christian terms—so that cosmology was founded in the biblical doctrine of creation, theology, and theodicy in the doctrine of the Father and his Logos, ethics, and psychology in the doctrines of sin and grace—a process of intellectual transfusion occurred whereby Christianity was enabled to replace metaphysics as the supreme intellectual system of the West. . . . The creeds and the dogmas which were originally forged to defend Christian identity against absorption by Hellenistic currents of thought and religiosity, became after Nicea the instruments of the exclusive establishment of Christianity as the true philosophy abrogating all others. . . . Dogma may have been counter-metaphysical insofar as it preserved the identity of faith against metaphysical absorption; but by its emphasis on definition and certitude and its claim to be treated as a first principle dogma betrayed its own purpose and became the instrument of the strongest assumption of a metaphysical identity by the Christian faith.[27]

The matter was not improved either with the switch from Greek to the more tightly logical medium of Latin where the doctrines of the early fathers "were assembled in a rather petri-fied system, in which the margin of vagueness or mystery they retained in Greek was mercilessly lopped away."[28] The influence of Augustine here was powerful. Metaphysics under him became the ground plan for all experience: "a systematic geography of love and desire, joy and suffering, sin and virtue."[29] There was in the Christian West ultimately but one religious vocabulary, the terminology of Augustine's Latin, geared to control and hold all movements of the Spirit within its concepts:

Thus in whichever direction one pursued either religious experience or theological speculation after Augustine one came up against the all-embracing structures of his ground plan, which seemed the definitive institution of the boundaries of Christian truth. Nor could an escape be found through a return to Scripture, since Scripture was automati-cally read (even by the Reformers) through Augustinian eyes.[30]

The relevance of these observations for a depth understanding of religious life and the interpretation of the vows will, I hope, become evident in the succeeding chapters. For the present we might end this brief as well as somewhat complex reflection on the reasons for our "forgetfulness" of the earliest traditions—our seeming separation from our roots—with one further and also deeply alarming observation by O'Leary: "If the Church today is vulnerable to the critiques of Marx, Freud, and Nietzsche," he points out, "it is largely because of an Augustin-ianism insufficiently overcome." He sees this as a "metaphysical institutionalization of the Gospel which does not allow it to de-ploy its liberative challenge in concrete interplay with social and psychological situations, but tries to inscribe its message in a systematic code."[31] The pertinence of this insight for religious seems obvious, especially after the long and often painful strug-gle many of us just experienced in seeking approval for our con-stitutions as expressions of our lived experience and of our hopes. Whenever liberation language and concern for justice *threatens* the establishment, it has become top heavy. O'Leary in-sists (and this is certainly not new to any of us at this point) that for an authentic living of the Gospel today we need to "overcome metaphysics." We need to return to the roots, to open up to new paradigms in order to allow Christianity to become credible once again for our age. It is clear that contemporary liberation theologians—those concerned with the equality and dignity of women and of any other oppressed group, Christian ecologists and those who with them proclaim the goodness of all creation, as well as mystics everywhere—strongly agree with these observations. We are concerned here, it seems to me, with an ecclesial equivalent of Newtonian physics and our responsibility as God's people to think beyond its absolutes into our beginnings—into the energy of the Christian tradition as it emerged in its earliest times. If James J. Bacik is right and contemporary society is experiencing an "eclipse of mystery,"[32] then it will be our task to open ourselves up once more to the possibility of its reappearance. Nothing less than that is worthy of our heritage.

In the world of physics the quantum theory did this for scientists. It exposed them to mystery beyond Newtonian "solutions." Its discovery took them not only through a profound intellectual crisis, but also involved them in the intense emotional and existential experience of reality as paradoxical, as fundamentally dynamic and organic. This, because of its revolutionary difference from previous assumptions, almost led them to despair.[33] To accept reality as essentially paradoxical necessitates a radical shift in one's attitude. One must learn to approach it with different questions. The one-sided certainty of a mechanistic, dualistic worldview no longer holds and a holistic, ecological approach seems much more meaningful. "The spirit no longer appears to us an intruder in the realm of matter; we begin to suspect that we should rather welcome it," writes James Jeans, while Lincoln Barnet postulates "an ultimate, undiversified, and eternal ground beyond which there appears to be nowhere to progress."[34] The biologist Adolf Portman speaks of a " 'non-spatial abyss of mystery' which opens out behind the living organism, or at its origin."[35]

Taking our cue from the world of science, we might, in our quest for a new paradigm, begin with a surrender to the mystery. Our answers, we are told, will not come in calculable clarity, and we remember John Shea's promise that our experience will be one of ambiguity, of "exceeding darkness" as well as "undeserved light." The depth spirituality, which we are seeking as we return to our roots within an atmosphere of open rather than blind faith and attempt to think into our myths there, will be one with no final solutions. Questions will most likely lead to deeper questions as intellect yields precedence to heart and we, in our thinking, leave room for the existential and experiential; for the mystical, the paradoxical.

Toward a Holistic Paradigm

We have already certain indications of the milieu from which holistic spirituality arises: From our earliest traditions in the Jesus movement we know that God is essentially lover, nurturer, parent. The mystics who kept this insight experientially alive throughout the history of the church expand it for us. They draw their understanding of divine love quite naturally from their own experience of authentic self-giving. Love, they tell us, is love only if expressed toward another. No one can love in isolation. Love in its very essence speaks of outreach, of otherness, of sharing. God's love cannot be different here, only infinitely more so. In its reaching out for the other it, therefore, almost of necessity "breaks out" into creation. Creation is the love act of God.

The terms the German mystic Eckhart uses to describe this divine activity are filled with the exuberance and energy of the *dabhar*, the divine Word: In God's "pleasuring-forth" the universe, God is the "great underground river that no one can dam up and no one can stop." The divine creator "finds joy and rapture in us." The lover of humankind is "ever green, ever verdant, ever flowering. Every action of God is new. . . . God is the newest thing there is; the youngest thing there is. God is the beginning. . . . God is voluptuous and delicious."[36] For Hildegard of Bingen "all creation is gifted with the ecstasy of God's light." God is "the resounding Word, the It-Shall-Be." Poetically reflecting on God's creative activity she hears God speak: "With my mouth I kiss my own chosen creation. I uniquely, lovingly, embrace every image I have made out of the earth's clay."[37] A more contemporary mystical experience has T. S. Eliot refer to God's creative energy as a "dance at the still point," drawing our attention to God's dynamic paradox:

> At the still point of the turning world. Neither flesh nor
>   fleshless;
> Neither from nor towards; at the still point,
>   there the dance is.
> But neither arrest nor movement. And do not call it fixity.
> Where past and future are gathered. Neither movement from
>   nor towards,
> Neither ascent nor decline. Except for the point,
>   the still point,
> There would be no dance, and there is only the dance.
> I can only say, there we have been; but I cannot say where.
> And I cannot say, how long, for that is to place it in time.[38]

In God's divine act of love infinite diversity becomes manifest: "Everything that is is bathed in God, is enveloped by God, who is round-about us all, enveloping us. Being is God's circle and in this circle all creatures exist. Everything that is in God is God."[39] Holiness, therefore, pervades creation. "And God saw that it was good"(Gen. 1:4, 10, 12, 18, 21, 25, 31). God's creation is God's echo, an act of infinite wisdom, grace, and playful joy: "from of old I was poured forth. . . . I [wisdom] was God's delight day by day, playing before God all the while, playing on the surface of God's earth; and I found delight in the children of humankind" (Prov. 8:23, 30, 31).

The perspective I am here describing may appear new and perhaps foreign to some, but is, as I mentioned already, quite rooted in our earliest traditions. When one reads the creation accounts, much depends on where one wishes to place the emphasis. Thus, a God rejoicing at the goodness of all is simply a God not frequently mentioned in dualistic spirituality, which chooses to place its emphasis elsewhere; but one can hardly deny the fact that in Scripture this God is duly represented. Incidentally, the same God of the first creation account cited above is also the God beyond patriarchal dualism, if one allows oneself to see this: "God created man in his image; in the divine image God created him; *male and female God created them*" (Gen. 1:27). The image of God cannot be contained in one-sidedness. Elsewhere I have discussed the attempts to do precisely that, to suppress the God of diversity (symbolically at home in both genders) through the translation of the term *Elohim* (used for

God in this text and composed of a feminine plural with a masculine suffix) in purely masculine terms.[40] Scripture was written
and is read by human beings. The writers were inspired, yes, but
were writing *within* a culture and worldview. To understand and
appreciate the Word necessitates knowledge of this and critical
reappraisal at every turn in the human journey. "No text written
by human beings is without its shadow side, which the passage
of time may throw into deeper relief. Theology is largely a
struggle with these shadows."[41]

Now, if creative love cannot be contained in one-sidedness,
neither ought the human being that issues forth from God be
divided against him or herself. For Eckhart the human being is
essentially the love response to the divine; the one who in a mul-
titude of ways gathers God's infinite diversity in worship and in
praise; the one in whom the universe is brought to word, to
prayer, to meaning; the psalmist in whom all of creation praises
God; the mirror in whom God is reflected back to God; the
virgin mother whose emptiness receives God in releasement and
births God back to God in gratitude;[42] the spark where in the
eternity of time and the infinity of space the love of God breaks
forth, lights up, bursts into song:

God is always flowing into the soul and can never escape the soul. But
the soul can easily escape God. As long, however, as a person remains
under God, that person receives the unmediated divine influx. . . .
The masters say that the soul receives as a light from light.[43]

Seize God in all things, for God is in all things.[44]

The prophet says: "The Lord has stretched forth his hand" (Jr.1:9).
And he means by that the Holy Spirit. Now he goes on to say: "He
has touched my mouth" and means by this that "he has spoken to me"
(Jr. 1:9). The mouth of the soul is the highest part of the soul and this
is meant by saying "He has put his word in my mouth" (Jr. 1:9). That
is the kiss of the soul: there mouth comes to mouth; there the Father
gives birth to the Son in the soul, and there is where the soul is
addressed.[45]

The tenderness and passion of these passages is striking. Sue
Woodruff, writing on Mechtild of Magdeburg, Eckhart's fore-
mother, identifies similar themes:

She touches on themes as old as the book of Job, the Psalms, the Song of Songs. Her writings abound in images of light, fire, reflection, love, longing. She sees the soul in these images and God in the same images. We are the spark; God is the fire. We are the fire; God is the light. We are the light; God is the moon. We are the moon; God is the sun. We are the sun; God is love. We are love; God is compassion. We are compassionate; we resemble God.[46]

The call of the mystics is a call to creative fidelity; to a response out of a diversity of gifts, in utter releasement, for the glory of God. "We—body, soul, male, female, young, old—mirror the splendor of creation. We are the ground, the humus, where the God-seed can germinate, root and flower forth in our day."[47] But we can also choke this seed and thwart the creative effort of God. If the primary virtue in this holistic approach to our traditions is surrender to the creative activity of God in and through me; if I am called to releasement—the creative letting-go of personal presuppositions, assumptions, expectations, prejudices, in order to let be what is as it is in its original divine intent—then the primary vice is precisely the refusal to do this. The will to power refuses to let God be God in creation. It blinds itself to the giver and posits itself as the origin of meaning, imposing concepts, personal projections, and interpretations on others and even on the self. I call it the *Cartesian affliction*: "I think, therefore, *it is*." Rather than allowing divinity to be born in one's depths, one imposes it on oneself and lords it over others; one dominates the world. "Why is it," asks Eckhart, "that some people do not bear fruit? It is because they are so busy clinging to their egotistical attachments."[48]

The self-emptying required for creative authenticity is one of the primary themes in the Gospels. But it is, I believe, never simply recommended for the sake of emptiness itself, but always in order to be filled. The "virgin womb" is significant in its emptiness only because it is ready to receive life and to bear it forth once again into the heart of God.[49] We empty ourselves to find ourselves—our wholeness, our authenticity, our freedom—in the love of God.

In contemporary thought an echo of these themes of divine love and human surrender is beautifully found in Rahner's theology of grace. Grace, for Rahner, is the living presence of

God—God's indwelling within the human person. Human beings are destined for God and gifted with a unique openness toward this end from the moment of their creation. The presence
of God pervades their being. They are transcendence, an active
openness (though not always conscious of this) to the infinite
and absolute.

God wishes to communicate himself [herself], to pour forth the love
which [s/he] himself [herself] is. That is the first and the last of his
[her] real plans and hence of his [her] real world too. Everything else
exists so that this one thing might be: the eternal miracle of infinite
Love. And so God makes a creature whom [s/he] can love: [s/he] creates man [woman]. [S/He] creates him [her] in such a way that [s/he]
can receive this love which is God himself [herself], and that [s/he] can
and must at the same time accept it for what it is: the ever astounding
wonder, the unexpected, unexacted gift.[50]

We are at all times "addressed and claimed" by God's love. We
are in fact created for it—we are loved into being for the sake of
Love. This call moves beyond membership in any institutional
church. It belongs to humankind. God's self-communication is
"offered to all and fulfilled in the highest way in Christ." It is
"the goal of all creation." It stamps and determines our nature
so that a rejection of it brings us into profound contradiction
with our deepest being. Whenever we truly and completely accept ourselves, we are held in God's grace for it already speaks
within us.[51]

Limit-situations, where the call beyond is felt especially
keenly in the here and now, are where Rahner localizes the experience of grace with particular poignancy.

Grace is operative in the experience of infinite longings, of radical optimism, of unquenchable discontent, of the torment of the insufficiency of everything attainable, of the radical protest against death, the
experience of being confronted with an absolute love precisely where it
is lethally incomprehensible and seems to be silent and aloof, the experience of a radical guilt and of a still-abiding hope, and so on. These
elements are in fact tributary to that divine force which impels the created spirit—by grace—to an absolute fulfillment.[52]

One is reminded here of Eckhart's observation: "the divine
countenance is capable of maddening and driving all souls out of

their senses with longing for it. When it does this . . . it is
thereby drawing all things to itself. . . . Every creature—
whether it knows it or not—seeks repose."[53]

And yet the will to power persists and with it sin and alienation. Our unwillingness to recognize the goodness in which we
are held and to respond with releasement and gratitude has
brought us already from the first moment of creation into radical contradiction with our roots, our deepest self. We stand in
need of redemption—to be re-membered into the Christ, God's
love incarnate. This, then, is our salvation: the love of God in
our midst, who came to show us our way home into the heart of
God; who became human so that we might be divinized—returned into our own depths where God is.

Holistic spirituality sees eternal life as already begun and as
realized ever more by our moving into the Christ event in which
we are already held. What matters is *vision* and our *living into that
vision*. With the early Christians we see Jesus as the Wisdom of
God, the "child of Sophia sent to announce that God is the God
of the poor and heavy laden, of the outcasts and those who suffer injustice."[54] Our salvation, then, lies in compassion. "Those
who follow compassion find life for themselves, justice for their
neighbor, and glory for God."[55] They live in the fullness of
time. The redemptive task of Jesus was precisely to show us
this. His suffering and death cannot be understood in cultic
terms, as atonement for sin, nor was it understood that way in
the earliest Jesus tradition, though this interpretation soon took
over.[56] The God whom Jesus came to proclaim did not need or
desire restitution. "Jesus' execution, like John's, result[ed] from
his mission and commitment as prophet and emissary of the
Sophia-God"[57] who holds open a future for the broken and rejected, and offers God's gracious goodness unconditionally to
all. Jesus was killed by the ruling powers of his day because of
his freedom and the integrity toward which he called his followers. When freedom encounters the need to control, power will
always rise up and try to destroy it.

This interpretation of Jesus' death in no way lessens its redemptive character, nor for that matter does it need to do away
with the view that Jesus "took on sin," "died for our sins," and
so forth; for was not the very sin that crucified him—the will to

power, to control, to dominate, to oppress—the sin of the world that needed to be overcome? And here also lies the power of the resurrection, for in it sin and its dominance was nullified. The "abandoned" prophet was raised and his message vindicated, namely, that the Lover-God will not be denied and that the freedom that this opens up for God's people is real. God has loved us with an everlasting love. We are precious to God; we are the beloved of God; we are held in the palm of God's hand. Any oppressive imagery of God and its concomitant guilt died with Jesus. As Paul tells us: "We have been released from the law— for we have died to what bound us—and we serve in the new spirit, not the antiquated letter" (Rom. 7:6). And later: "The law of the spirit, the spirit of life in Christ Jesus, has freed you from the law of sin and death" (Rom. 8:2).[58]

Sebastian Moore in a poetic meditation on the redemptive power of the resurrection expresses these thoughts powerfully in the words of a disciple who has encountered the risen Christ out of, and within, the experience of emptiness left by his death:

I think, in retrospect, that I saw him *with* that emptiness I spoke of, as though the emptiness were a kind of second sight. . . .

Since then, life has consisted in growing in the vision. Not without words—exciting new words which, we know, are changing forever the religious universe. God is this man. This man had come to epitomize finally all our hope and all our emptiness; and when that space became alive God became alive. God is this man in us. . . . We have come into this man and feel with his heart and look through those eyes. God we know as Spirit, as the heart of that equation between God and life which no religiousness ever quite dares to make for fear of losing touch with guilt. As we have now! It is all washed away by the blood which we now drink.[59]

In Christ Jesus we stand in the fullness of time *loved*. Our salvation consists in moving ever more authentically into this vision and bodying it forth existentially through compassion.

It is clear that the dualistic-patriarchal tradition to which all of us are accustomed may find the above reflection disturbing. It has, from the beginning of its contact with Christianity, laid stress on the fact that our redemption needed to be won in the face of a deity whose wrath demanded to be placated by human/

divine sacrifice and that Jesus' crucifixion paid the "price" for our being reinstated into divine favor. Through it we interpreted the agony of the garden, to mention just one example, not as a struggle with one's own integrity in the face of persecution, but as a struggle with patriarchal decrees. Through it we saw the gates of heaven thrown open with the last drop of blood shed in bloody atonement. It may be difficult and emotionally upsetting for some to shed this image. Thinking critically into our myths often can be just that. The question we need to ask ourselves, however, is whether such an interpretation, given our above meditation on the salvific will of God, is in fact even plausible. Does an *Abba* demand crucifixion? No human parent who truly loves his or her child would. Why must we, then, contort our own understanding of love with such an interpretation of God's, and reassure ourselves and others, in the face of doubt, by relegating it all to the "divine mystery beyond our experience."

The experience of a dualistic-patriarchal world, which was ultimately responsible for introducing the cultic dimension into Christianity, was of fatherhood in a general *paterfamilias* context where life and death decisions over children were the patriarch's prerogative. This no longer is our understanding of fatherhood and parenting. Why, then, must we persist in using these concepts for God? Besides, as I have suggested above, this was also not the interpretation of Jesus who worked hard at bringing the mercy and tenderness of God into our experience. If we are held in the unconditional love of God from the moment of creation, why should the God of sinners be any different from the "prodigal" father of the parable, or from the shepherd looking for his sheep, or from the woman who lost a silver piece (Luke 15), or from numerous other examples of forgiveness and compassion that Jesus presented to us? Why would Jesus even have told these stories if he had not intended them to be representative of his God? Sandra Schneiders in analyzing the parable of the Prodigal Son speaks explicitly to this issue: "In the parable of the prodigal son (Lk 15:11–32) Jesus presents the fatherhood of God as the very antithesis of patriarchy." While the older son through his unquestioning obedience and loyalty is the perfect spokesperson for the patriarchal structure, "his younger brother, by assuming autonomy, has rebelled against the very principle of patriarchy according to which there is only one adult in any family."[60] The father, according to Jesus, sides with the younger son. Just as he had enabled his earlier rebellion and quest to venture forth on his own, so now he not only refuses to punish him but in fact rejoices at his return. He rejects the older son's demands for vindication—a "patriarchal principle"—and will not "hear" the younger son's offer to reenter the patriarchal household as a servant in restitution for his offense.[61] The father sees the younger son as he has always seen him, as his *beloved* son.

God's forgiving love, not human evil, determines God's relationship to humanity. The father, far from asserting patriarchal superiority and privilege, seems to recognize the younger son as his equal, i.e., as an adult. To the father the son's return to the household, like his leaving, is an act of adult freedom. The relationship between them is not one of offended domination to rebellious submission but of freely offered love asking and accepting love in return. The prodigal son, like the sinful woman who entered the house of Simon to wash Jesus' feet (Lk 7:36–50), is one in whom loving repentance and loving forgiveness meet in total defiance of the patriarchal model of justification through law.[62]

The God of Jesus, our God, is infinite compassion and love. We are drawn into God through Christ Jesus. As we assume responsibility for the Christification of ourselves and of the world, Christ's incarnation continues in us. Our call is to let God be God in us; to surrender our will to dominate in grateful releasement. This is why God became human: to show us how to live; how to fulfill our destiny as lovers of God and of each other; how to find our way back to authenticity. In the death and resurrection of Jesus, God triumphed over all sin—our willful rejection of our own integrity. In Christ all things are made whole; all things are made new. Holistic spirituality invites us to take seriously this Good News and to make it our own.

Conclusion

We live in the turning point, in an age of crisis where the dualism of our past no longer empowers or gives life, and where a more ancient tradition calls us to remember. Who our God is, who we are, and how we are related in authenticity, are questions that may not remain speculative any longer. We are asked to live into our myths with the passionate involvement of our very existence. Ours is the choice. We can either wither in the drought and die of dehydration, or face the challenge of "our quiet little house" with all the terror that this may initially bring, and thus move into new life.

The journey through this chapter may have been arduous at times. I did not intend this to be discouraging, however, but rather presented it in the hope of providing a necessary backdrop for our subsequent reflections on the vowed life. Never so much as now in my own life, in my studies, and in my own reflective experience, have I been convinced of the need to make choices—personal and communal decisions—that are supported by wider perspectives than merely one's here and now, or even one's community traditions and specific mandate, one's personal or group interests in immediate issues of the present, important though they may be. Today we are impacted globally and find ourselves within a space-time continuum that makes simple cause and effect decisions laughable. We can no longer trust ourselves to current ways of doing or seeing things—trends, be they psychological or theological or sociological—without thoroughly probing into their "why"; nor can we simply make provisional decisions for the sake of getting the job done, without looking at the wider implications.

Today, living into our baptism through the vows moves us far beyond the given set of rules or constitutions that affect us personally or congregationally. Our very existence is at stake: the credibility of Gospel living and personal maturation through religious commitment. Can women and men become whole as vowed members of a religious congregation in the late twentieth century? Is our life a viable Christian option for our time? Without some depth perspective on the crisis that affects our century's worldview generally and Christian self-understanding in particular, I do not believe we can answer these questions either adequately or meaningfully no matter how strongly we believe in an affirmative response. This chapter's discussion of dualism and of a possible holistic Christian response to it was intended to prepare us for this task in the considerations that follow; to provide, if you will, the soil for the hidden treasure we seek as we turn now to the particular task of reflecting on living the vows in an age of change.

Questions for Focus, Reflection, Discussion

1. Do you see religious life in our time suffering from what Jean Shinoda Bolen identifies as a "drought mentality"? How so?

2. How, in your experience of our culture, our church, and religious life, can you identify the relation between dualism, hierarchism, and patriarchy?

3. What is your reaction to the invitation to think into our myths? Does it excite or frighten you? Why?

4. To which paradigm of spirituality do you see yourself belonging, the dualistic model or the holistic one? Why?

5. Have you, in your personal experiences, ever encountered a limit-situation? Are the descriptions by Bernard Boelen and John Shea realistic?

6. What is your reaction to the teachings of the early Jesus movement and the understanding of church as *basileia*?

7. Was your attitude to church dogma and doctrine affected by this chapter's discussion of the missionary movement in the early church and the effects of Greek metaphysics on the formulations of our beliefs? If so, how?

8. What in the holistic paradigm do you find most difficult to accept? What do you find most liberating?

2

What Matters Is Vision

In the first chapter of Brennan Manning's *The Wisdom of Accepted Tenderness* he explains that "all changes in the quality of a person's life must grow out of a change in his [her] vision of reality."[1] The holistic approach to spirituality of the preceding pages attempted to offer just that: a new paradigm, an alternate vision of reality from the one that has dominated our perception for centuries.

1. God's reign is realized in our midst, we said, yet is also still in process, calling us to accept and live into the fullness of time.

2. The Christian community is a "discipleship of equals"—of friends—all of whom are loved and are gifted in diversity and for the glory of God.

3. Creation—all of it—is holy and needs to be encountered as such.

4. We are the breakthrough of God's creative activity and are called to respond to it in releasement and gratitude.

5. Original sin is our refusal of this call, this heritage. It is the will to domination, the will to power.

The question that now concerns us is how this new paradigm, this alternate vision, might affect the quality of our lives as religious; what it can offer us and of what it will ask us to let go as we attempt to live and to draw meaning from our vows and the religious life that flows from them.

Most of us would agree, I think, that the dualistic paradigm of our recent past created in us a tendency to reduce any reflection on the vows to an identification and explanation of what we promise and what we subsequently do or do not do to live

35

up to the evangelical counsels or the "consecrated life." We all too readily, I am sure, remember the list of regulations that we memorized in our early years of training and which still to this day haunt some of us at various times. Much of the prescriptive legislation of canon law regarding the hierarchy of governance or concerning the disposal of property in our present "approved" constitutions is also a reminder of this dualistic mind-set and vision. The concern that arises for us within a holistic perspective, however, goes beyond the "oughts" of *doing* and invites us rather to probe into *who* we are and *how* we are *as vowed*. It asks what it means to *be* vowed, to *be* consecrated. It stresses vowed life as a way of *being*—a disposition—leaving the dimension of prescription or prohibition on a secondary plain, safe in the knowledge that the latter must flow from the former or ultimately perish for lack of energy and motivation. It cannot be externally imposed and remain life-giving.

No Longer Set Apart

What, then, does it mean to be consecrated by vow? At this point of our reflection it is clear, I believe, that a holistic paradigm can no longer accept a view of consecration that implies "having been set apart," or a life-style that encourages this concept. Because Jesus came to proclaim the holiness of all creation, the holiness, therefore, of every human being, because in this way he affirmed our universal mandate to give glory to God simply by being *who we are*, no one needs to be set apart. The world as the breakthrough of God's creative energy is sacred. God, through the incarnation, shows us that there is no division between the world here and the world "above." As God becomes human, humans enter into the divine. There is, therefore, no need for the individual or group to be "consecrated"—in the sense of being made "superior"—in order to bridge the abyss between the sacred and the secular. We—all of us—are called into solidarity, into intimacy with God in Christ; called also, because of that, to cosmic hospitality. Sandra Schneiders speaks clearly to this new vision:

In the synoptic gospels Jesus insists that nothing that is created remains profane; nothing requires to be set apart but only to be used rightly (cf.

Mk. 7:1–23). The Sabbath is for humans, not humans for the Sabbath (Mk. 2:27). The veil of the Holy of Holies is rent as men and women are drawn into the heart of God by the sacrifice of Jesus (Mt. 27:51). A simple meal of friendship between Jesus and his disciples replaces all sacrifices. . . .

. . . [C]onsecration in the community of the New Testament involves neither separation nor superiority. . . . To be consecrated is to be holy, to be united with God in the love poured forth in our hearts by the Holy Spirit of Jesus (cf. Rom. 5:5). . . . We have been sent into the world as Jesus was sent into the world—to bring salvation by solidarity with, not by separation from, those to whom we are sent.[2]

Taking vows, therefore, can no longer be interpreted in terms of making more sacred what already is sacred. It simply cannot mean anything different from what Jesus declared all of creation to be. All of life is holy and it might be easier for us if we were to understand different vocations as complementary calls to contextualize and bear witness to this holiness, rather than to interpret them "above or below each other" on the hierarchical ladder. In the light of our holistic approach, then, it will make more sense to see religious vows as one sees matrimonial vows: both give a particular shape to, and address a particular way of living out, our baptismal consecration.[3] Thus, through our choice to live celibately in community, as sharing with and listening to one another, we bring our baptismal consecration to maturity in a different way than, but not in a superior way to, others who choose to work out their consecration in other ways.

Religious and other Christians are equally called to witness to the infinite love of God, but the richness of that mystery requires a variety of expressions. The witness different Christians are called to give is not distinguished by location on a scale of comparative excellence but by the aspects of the mystery of divine love which come to special expression in their various lifestyles. The witness of each Christian vocation is rich but limited; therefore, adequate witness to the mystery of divine love can only be given in mutuality and complementarity.[4]

Because of our inherent finitude, none of us can fully contain and give witness to the breakthrough of God in creation. Each one of us as we live our calling with authenticity is, therefore, a partial but valid expression of the multidimensional manifestation of God's self-revelation in Christ.

The vision presented here points directly to the *basileia* of the early Jesus movement, which we discussed in the preceding chapter. As Christians we are a community of equals before a loving God who has gifted us in diverse but complementary ways and calls us to be for each other out of these gifts, in gratitude and praise. "The humility by which we simultaneously realize both our limitation and our giftedness opens us to an appreciation of the mutuality of witness in the church."[5] Dualistic distinctions that easily arise out of a need to be the "greatest" in God's eyes, will thus give way to genuine celebration as we, in Sandra Schneider's words, "rejoice in the shared poverty which establishes us in the lowest place," and has us find solidarity there with all Christians and even with Jesus himself "who is among us, meek and humble of heart, as one who serves."[6]

The implications of this perspective for ministry and mission, as well as for congregational life especially in terms of governance and the initial incorporation of newer members, are interesting. For starters, it would seem that religious who truly accept the "community of equals" will find it less difficult to let go of long cherished congregational ministries and will accept, even enable, the birthing of a church that transcends the distinctions of lay, religious, and cleric; where people serve according to their talents, not their "state." Catholic schools or hospitals are, after all, not more Catholic because sisters, brothers, or priests run them or work in them. Nor do Catholics have an edge on what is truly Christian. "Defensive separation from the world, and an unconsciously complacent conviction of specialness in the church," as Sandra Schneiders puts it, "must give way to an embrace of all that is human and a cherishing of our solidarity—not only with Christians but with all people."[7]

The welcoming and the incorporation of new members into religious life will, I believe, also be affected when the *basileia* vision of a community of equals truly takes hold among us. It is my hope to address this issue in a separate chapter later. For the present, suffice it to say that the community of equals begins with the first letter of inquiry written by a newer member to the congregation, and endures throughout the many years of introduction and incorporation until final vows and beyond. All

forms of exclusivism and elitism, from the subtlest to the most
blatant, will need to be addressed critically and radically here.
This is not an easy task, for most of them are imbedded in the
very structure of incorporation ("formation") itself. It almost
universally speaks of the hierarchical that has been with us for
thousands of years as a cultural phenomenon.

Perhaps on the symbolic level it would help to see the needed
shift from a dualistic to a holistic incorporation process as similar to moving from an imitation of the structured initiation rites
of young men in primitive cultures to accepting the more organic movement into maturity of the young women in these
same cultures. Persons do not have to be put through a "trial" to
prove their belonging or their fitness (no matter how "hard" we
had it "when we were novices"). The gift for community and
religious life (as was the gift of womanhood in the young
woman of primitive times) is found within and comes forth
from those so called in due time. Our development here, if it is
authentic, is organic—from the womb of our inner selves, the
cycle of our own growth. It need not be imposed or artificially
tested but requires nurturance within a communal setting sensitive to this. Furthermore, we can no longer expect from newer
members what we ourselves are not willing to live. No amount
of evaluations and external authority, no matter how subtle or
disguised, will bring this about. When they ask us, "friends,
where do you live?" with Jesus we must answer: "come and
see." And what they see will have to be *who we are—all of us.*
No person in charge, nor any hand-picked community, can suc-
cessfully model the ideal religious life that the members are not
living. Nor for that matter ought they to "model" the life the
members *are* living for we are all in this together, co-responsible.
New members come to join *us.* It is the community (all of us,
not merely a select group) that must welcome them in word and
in deed, for it is the community with which they will spend the
rest of their lives. The "hothouse" mentality of "initial formation" simply does not represent this community any longer, nor
does this mentality do enough to challenge members to be truly
brother and sister to those who come to join us.

In the last several years we have done much to address the
vocation crisis afflicting many of our congregations. My ex-

perience with these efforts has been as a teacher in one of the intercommunity novitiate programs in the mid-west where I interacted with newer members for some seven years. Not being a member of a "formation" team and, therefore, to some extent as an outsider looking in, I gained the impression that many of our ever-changing policies regarding incorporation are more like desperate attempts at patchwork than truly holistic and revolutionary revisions. In the unprecedented rethinking of religious life demanded of us by a paradigm shift of the magnitude we are here discussing for this age and culture, nothing short of the radical will do. We remember Brennan Manning: all authentic changes in the quality of our lives must grow out of a change in our vision of reality. We need to return to the roots. Our deepest roots are found in putting on the mind and heart of Christ Jesus and embracing the foundational vision of his *basileia*.

The effects that a view of universal giftedness and mutuality of witness in a community of equals will have on congregational governance are somewhat complex and easily open to misinterpretation. A later chapter dealing with authority and obedience will probe more deeply into this issue. For now one simple clarification may be all that is necessary: We all know that to be gifted in a community of equals does not mean to be equally gifted. Just as all of us are called but not all of us are called to the same life-style or ministry, so all of us are gifted but not all with same gifts. Leadership, the empowerment of the group to be about its call, is a gift. It is a needed gift wherever people are gathered together toward a common end. Discernment of gifts for the good of the group is a community responsibility and the choice of leadership ought to be precisely that. Our gifts are ours for service. Authority is not antithetical, therefore, to a community of equals but must be viewed by, and called forth in, the group not as elevation, but as service. Nor are these observations to be viewed as a return to hierarchy hidden behind the smoke screen of the word "service." (Hierarchs, after all, have been the "servants of the servants of God" for centuries.) Those, however, who are held in the breakthrough of God know, above all else, that all of life is surrender to self-emptying and thus to freedom. They stand in the freedom of their own inner authority that directs their vision and, from this vision, all their actions toward service and mutual empowerment as they experience membership in the body. They call forth and allow themselves to be called forth on various levels of communal involvement. Diversity of gifts does not mean hierarchy of gifts, hence there also is no hierarchy of service.

Although this appears self-evident, and most of us have heard or said similar things, it is my sense that in the living-out of this vision we often are still plagued by a hidden dualistic hierarchism. What, for example, is the reason behind the seeming need in many congregations to have almost all community offices, boards, committees, and task forces open to all—to all volunteers who wish to "serve"? This policy tends to eliminate any meaningful discernment of gifts—any discernment and calling forth by the group. Could it be possible that a hidden and often unconscious motivation for this policy really lies in a sense of inadequacy and a need for inclusion on the part of the membership coupled with resentment of those truly gifted in one or other area of service whose presence—possibly by request— would foster a perceived elitism? Persons gifted to serve in various areas, such as community life, government planning, facilitation, and the like, can, of course, do the job more efficiently and speedily, but they are fewer in number than the volunteers; hence they *appear* special. This is so mainly because in a dualistic paradigm the value of the function is, because of misplaced abstraction, identified with the value of the person performing it, raising and lowering the individual's dignity accordingly. Equality of persons is viewed as dependent upon the right of all to do all regardless of their gifts. Since we are all called, so the argument goes, we should all be allowed to do anything we want to volunteer for. Often chaos, not true inclusion, is the consequence of such a way of thinking, and the inadequacy of service that is the result frequently collapses the agency or committee from within, ultimately leading to no service at all.

Essential for an authentic, holistic paradigm is the internalization of the fact that God breaks out in diversity and that discernment of this breakthrough, both personal and communal, is mandated for true and life-giving creativity. This vision is described beautifully by Beatrice Bruteau as she challenges our

culture to a revolution of consciousness, "participatory consciousness," as she calls it:

When I love with participatory consciousness, I see that what the other
is is some of my life-energy living there, and what I am is some of the
other's life-energy living here in me. I can no longer divide the world
into "we's" and "they's." I have an awareness of one large life circulat-
ing through all. In some way, my boundary has become less definite in
the sense of being less hard and sealed off. My selfhood has become
radiant, streaming out from me, and is found participating in the other
even as it is found in me. But I am not engulfed by an all-absorbing
unity in which my uniqueness is dissolved. Creative live is entirely the
protection and nurturance of personal freedom and uniqueness. It is
precisely because a person as a whole is absolutely unique that it transcends all the categories by which abstractive consciousness would
classify it. The single large life in which I participate is a community of
whole unique selves who freely form and constitute this large unifying
life by the intercommunication of their creative love energies. So, far
from being absorbed or dissolved, I feel that as a member of this community my interior sense of self-possession, or self-being, is more
intense and clearer, in the sense of being more luminous and more
truly "I."[8]

It is clear that nothing short of a revolution of consciousness will
bring about this kind of perception shift, which challenges all
jealousy, envy, over-againstness, authoritarianism, as well as
subservience. Nothing short of a revolution of consciousness, in
other words, will help us truly and unequivocally celebrate our
uniqueness and our giftedness while recognizing our need for the
services of others of which authentic authority is one—not a
greater one than the rest, just one among them.

The three examples discussed here, though I touched on them
only briefly, were intended to illustrate the transcending of dualism that a holistic paradigm necessitates: transcending the dichotomy of the sacred and the secular, of religious and laity;
transcending the split between the "ones who belong" and the
"ones who want to belong," between professed and "novices";
transcending the division between "superior" and "subordi-
nate." I will deal with many of these issues again. What needs to
be pointed out right now, however, is the fact that transcendence
does not at all imply "doing away with" or "eliminating" what

is being transcended. Authentic transcendence takes up into itself that beyond which it moves and transforms it. Thus, the secular is not done away with, but acknowledged in its sacredness, in its belonging to the holy, to the whole: "All things are yours, whether it be . . . the world, or life, or death, or the present, or the future: all these are yours, and you are Christ's, and Christ is God's" (1 Cor. 3:21–23). The transcendence in this citation from Corinthians is not of the world but of the "worldly"—of the boasting, of the will to power. Religious in contemporary society do not flee the world. Today the word is "immersion." With Eckhart we are called to be free in the world, free for the world, as well as free of it—of its power, its domination.[9] Transcendence lies not in the will to power, but in the will to surrender; not in flight, but in embracing and transforming.

If we move to the second example discussed above, I once again do not deny that the one who wants to belong is different from the one who already belongs; the new member from the older professed member. I simply suggest the transcending of destructive attitudes springing from the absolutization of dualism. This transcendence happens through genuine, sustained, and communal welcome; through the humility of our "shared poverty," of our striving *together* toward holiness by living the evangelical counsels in community; through our acknowledgment of each other's contributions and the legitimacy of felt needs; through mutual responsibility.

Finally, the distinction between gifts and the recognition of the gift of leadership, in particular, is maintained also in the holistic approach to community and governance. We accept the wisdom of the past even as we are transcending our past, for there is no time in history without profound insight. But the abuses of the "superior-inferior" syndrome and the misplaced elitism of our past dualistic mind-set is overcome. Transcendence lies in the acknowledgment, the celebration, of diverse gifts and in seeing our mutual call to service. Our passion is for the whole, the holy. We are about the reign of God, not our own. Again we must stress that the holistic as such does not oppose the dualistic, as if one were dealing with a simple logical contradiction where the truth of one premise eliminates the possibility of the other. The holistic, as a matter of fact, does not use logic as its essential language and is quite comfortable with paradox. It sees that mere opposition never leads to transcendence, but only gets caught in an atmosphere of conflict. There is, therefore, no "over-againstness" (though distinctions are maintained and diversity celebrated) in the holistic paradigm. It accepts the categories of the past if they empower life and creativity, but avoids all absolutizations. It simply sees with different eyes.

The Primacy of Disposition

Up to this point in my discussion I have laid special stress on what a holistic vision of vowed consecration can no longer accept and will have to move beyond. This led to reflection on the holistic response to dualism with examples of how such a response might affect our vision and our subsequent decisions and actions in specific areas of religious life. The question to which we must now turn brings us back to the beginning of this chapter and asks more directly how we as vowed religious can give shape to our baptismal consecration. A specific concern for me in this investigation revolves around our calling to give glory to God by becoming fully alive. How does religious life effect fullness of personhood? How can we work out our baptismal commitment toward full maturity and, therefore, indeed claim complementarity with sacramental matrimony by means of the vows we take?

I find that when these kind of questions are asked, the temptation is often most pressing to revert back to prescriptions and prohibitions in order to supply answers. It is interesting to note, for example, how in the drawing up of our new constitutions and directories many of us truly got involved and made a genuine effort to express our *lived* experience—a kind of existential testament as to *who we are*. Others, however, felt the need for and insisted on greater specificity. For some reason, whenever we delve into what we are and how we live, it seems to make some of us feel more secure if we can hold on to and point to details; if we can have the "nuts and bolts" of the vows, if you will, hammered out for us and written somewhere. Often we think that religious life would "work" better—maybe we would draw more members—if we had things more clearly put in black and white. Then too, of course, we could see who is truly poor, or chaste, or obedient.

It is my sense that in many of our discussions on these matters our emphasis is placed too heavily on *action*. Somehow it seems to escape us that authentic action is directly proportional to the disposition that inspires it. If the disposition is not ours, neither is the action. It may be automatic, coerced, performed through manipulation—"playing the game," as some call it—but unless what I do arises out of who I am, out of the integrity of my *being*, it is not mine. We are dealing here with issues of maturity that, as will be discussed later, are intimately connected with authentic obedience. For the present, let me simply reiterate that mature and personal choice flows from a mature and personal vision, perception, and disposition. The former is impossible without the latter. Therefore, if we spend a great deal of time discussing what we are doing, ought to do, resolve to do or not to do, we are wasting precious energy unless what is going on is held within a previously developed attitude that grounds our resolve and our actions. Nor does it help to come together first to agree on the attitude. Dispositions or attitudes are not "agreed upon" by consensus. They emerge from insight that is given to us as grace and then flows out of us. They might be discovered in honest dialogue but cannot be willed or resolved or changed either by persuasion or decree. "When insight happens," Heidegger tells us, "we are struck in our very being by the lightning flash of Being. In insight we *ourselves* are *gazed upon*."[10] Dispositions or attitudes emerge in a personality. They are intrinsically connected with the maturation process. A changing disposition, for example, can rarely be talked about or articulated. It appears *in* us rather than being formulated *by* us. It is an event—in the true meaning of the word as "coming out," "coming forth"—that lights up our entire personality from within. Often it even surprises us in our encounter with it: "I used to see things this way, but now I don't any longer, and I don't really know why," we will say, puzzled at the shift and whence it came.

It can, of course, be argued that membership in a particular congregation or, for that matter, membership in the Christian community presupposes the disposition upon which actions are based. But whereas there certainly is validity to this observation, what it ignores is precisely holistic growth. Babies too are baptized and are, therefore, members of the Christian community. This very fact speaks to the awareness (albeit often unconscious in a dualistic system) of the levels of openness on our journey into God. From the lengthy discussion in chapter 1 about paradigm shifts it has to be clear that not all Christians see the same realities in the same way. Religious are not exempt here. Our growth into depth varies. Even a common charism does not help change that fact. Diversity in religious life, in outlook, in values as well as ultimately in life-style, is a sensitive matter but it is a fact.

How, then, are we to address these issues? What can be said about the vows we take and the life-style that we embrace toward full maturity? It seems that any attempt to get some initial specificity has been thwarted. If discussion about actions—about what we do or should do—is useless unless a prior disposition is recognized and respected, and if this disposition is grace rather than resolve, emerging in time rather than allowing itself to be programed, there seems to be precious little left for us to say. And perhaps that is exactly how it should be. Perhaps it is precisely in not saying anything—in silence and in listening into that silence—that one begins to get insight into these questions. An exhortation of Karl Rahner comes to mind, one that he wrote in a brief essay of the 1970s entitled "Experiencing God," and one which I believe could easily be used as the leitmotif, the theme song, if you will, for a depth reflection on the vows:

Be still for once. Don't try to think of so many complex and varied things. Give . . . *deeper realities* of the spirit a chance now to rise to the surface: silence, fear, the ineffable longing for truth, for love, for fellowship, for God. Face loneliness, fear, imminent death! Allow such ultimate, basic human experiences *to come first*. Don't go talking about them, making up theories about them, but simply *endure these basic experiences.* . . .

If we do not learn slowly in this way to enter more and more into the company of God and to be open to him [her], if we do not constantly attempt to reflect in life primitive experiences of this kind—not deliberately intended or deliberately undertaken—and from that point

onwards to realize them more explicitly in the religious act of meditation and prayer, of solitude and the endurance of ourselves, . . . then
our religious life is and remains really of a secondary character and its
conceptual-thematic expression is false.[11]

What does it mean to live the vows; to consecrate one's life in
the spirit of poverty, celibate chastity, and obedience? What was
it that happened to us on that day when we spoke our commitment to God in the presence of our community? How did we
expect our lives to change with this commitment, and *are* they
changing because of it?

"Be still for once," Rahner urges us. Give the "deeper realities" a chance to surface: silence, fear, loneliness, longing for
truth, for love and companionship, for God. Don't make up theories about them. Rather, experience them; experience yourself,
each other, in the depth of who you are, for without this your
life is a sham, whereas *in it* the absolute awaits you.

A question that has become ever more urgent for me during
the last several years is precisely about the relationship between
these "deeper realities" and the vows. I have wondered for a
while now, and Rahner's reflection on how one experiences God
has intensified the question for me, whether perhaps our communal or ecclesial attempts to identify and articulate, to clarify,
enumerate, and define the hows and whats of our consecration
are not leading us dangerously close to losing its heart, its soul.

Rahner is very concrete and surprisingly experiential when he
describes what he means by these "deeper realities," the "depth
dimension," as I call them. His examples defy theorization.
They cannot be verified or categorized. They do not fit into the
question-answer format of a catechism, nor would they quite
find their way into a book on canon law. They ask, rather, more
questions than they give answers. They open up feelings, light
up memories, point to possibilities. They speak of life *lived*, of
pain endured, of passion and joy. They speak, in the truest sense,
of the Christ event, the very focus of our consecration:

Somewhere, someone seems to be weeping hopelessly. Someone
"packs it in" and knows—if [s/he] is now silent, if [s/he] is now patient, if [s/he] now gives in—that there is *nothing more* that *[s/he] could
seize on*, on which [s/he] could set his [her] hopes, that *this* attitude is

worthwhile. Someone enters into a final solitude where *no one* accompanies him [her]. Someone has the basic experience of being stripped even of his [her] very self. A [human being] as spirit in his [her] love for truth reaches—so to speak—the frontier of the absolute, . . . which sustains and is not sustained: . . . which is there even though we cannot reach out and touch it, which—if we talk about it—is again concealed behind our talk as its ground[12] [like disposition is to action].

The relationship of these "deeper realities" to the Holy may not be immediately clear. It is, in fact, more intuited than comprehended and often thinking about it hurts—deep down in the heart. That is why so many of us would rather dismiss it and prefer not to deal with it. It does not fit into our accustomed paradigm and therefore makes us feel uneasy. It lights up in stillness, in "being-with," rather than through words and explanations. It speaks indirectly of our vows—through loneliness and final solitude, through being stripped and the surrendering of power, through the enduring of silence and the thirst for truth. The acceptance of and dwelling in these "deeper realities" changes one's life. It leads to a change in vision, a change of attitude, and it is here, I believe, where their depth connection to the vows can best be experienced and touched.

What if, for just a brief moment, we would allow ourselves to think of the vows not as things or actions we promise to do or not to do, to give up, refrain from, or engage in? What if we saw them rather as dispositions that we embrace, as a way of being in which we dwell, as horizons which beckon us, as depths into which we commit ourselves to plunge on a lifelong journey into the silence and the simplicity that is God? What if we could let the vows light up for us not primarily as modes of action, but primarily as modes of perception—ways of seeing into which we grow, which enable us to encounter ourselves and the world on a deeper, on a sacred plane and, out of the vision won on that plane, lead us to action? What if we could permit ourselves to experience the vowed life as a spiral leading into an ever-deepening awareness of the holiness that is life (all of life with its pains and failures as well as its joys), of the sacredness that is creation, every aspect of creation? Would not then the prescriptive or regulatory concerns with which so many of us even today still approach discussions of the vowed life, and which so frequently distract us from the depth of holiness to which we are called, fade into the background, as theory yields to praxis? Would not then also those of us who have become disinterested, tired, and disenchanted with the entire legalistic and dualistic experience that the exploration into the vows has come to mean for us start to become involved again? Would not the vows begin to speak of life lived fully, of yearnings lying in the very heart of our humanity?

I have mentioned already that actions that evolve from visions flow on their own energy, whereas externally induced behavior quickly loses its power and vitality, and often can be maintained only through coercion by fear or guilt. What if we could accept the pronouncing of our vows as a commitment to the journey, to the process; as a trust-filled movement into possibilities, not as an accomplished fact that identifies us once and for all in a particular state of perfection that can be clearly measured, evaluated, and verified through predictable behavior? Would not then our strivings and our yearnings gain their rightful place in our life of consecration? And would not our evaluations individually and communally, instead of being merely success oriented, become truly Christlike: Much is forgiven him, her, us, because we have loved much.

The time is ripe at this point, I believe, to move from generalities to the specific. The discussions of the following chapters will attempt to do just that. We begin with a reflection on poverty and its meaning for us as an evangelical mandate. A meditation on celibacy will follow and, I hope, will shed light on the way we live together in community and commit ourselves to love one another. I will address some special concerns here, such as our relationship with each other within the context of the mid-life crisis and mid-life as such. I will look at the implications of this for community life: how our specific call to face our inner darkness, embrace intimacy needs, and face loneliness finds its shape there. Some thoughts on obedience and authority come next, to encourage us toward an appropriation of the depth dimension of leadership that transcends old "authority tapes" and moves us to authentic co-listening and responding as the questions of our times open for us ever-deeper questions and invite humble releasement as well as creativity. In conclusion I will consider our relationship with our newer members, our responsibility for new life, and the very real experience of death and resurrection to which living religious life in contemporary times calls us.

Questions for Focus, Reflection, Discussion

1. What is your reaction to the observation that holistic spirituality does not see consecration as "setting apart" but sees the entire world as God's creative breakthrough and, therefore, as sacred?

2. The complementarity of different vocations (i.e., matrimonial consecration and religious consecration) is also stressed in holistic spirituality. How does this perspective affect you? Are you comfortable with it?

3. How do you relate to the following observations:

"Catholic schools or hospitals are, after all, not more Catholic because sisters, brothers, or priests run them or work in them. Nor do Catholics have an edge on what is truly Christian."

With respect to community life and incorporation: "The community of equals [Christ's *basileia*] begins with the first letter of inquiry written by a newer member to the congregation, and endures throughout the many years of introduction and incorporation until final vows and beyond." (This does not mean, of course, that someone may not leave.)

Religious development, "if it is authentic, is organic—from the womb of our inner selves, the cycle of our own growth. It need not be imposed or artificially tested but requires nurturance within a communal setting sensitive to this."

"Leadership [is] the empowerment of the group to be about its call."

"Diversity of gifts does not mean hierarchy of gifts, hence there also is no hierarchy of service."

"In a dualistic paradigm the value of the function [i.e., leadership] is, because of misplaced abstraction, identified with the value of the person performing it, raising and lowering the individual's dignity accordingly," and often causing ambition, competition, jealousy, and politicking to disrupt community discernment.

Beatrice Bruteau's reflection on "participatory consciousness."

"Authentic action is directly proportional to the disposition that inspires it. If the disposition is not ours, neither is the action. It may be automatic, coerced, performed through manipulation—playing the game,' as some call it, but unless what I do arises out of who I am, out of the integrity of my *being*, it is not mine."

4. What is your reaction to the suggestion that any meaningful discernment on the vowed life needs to be preceded by the experience of silence, by the facing of loneliness, of our ultimate limits, of ourselves, of Rahner's "deeper realities"?

5. How do you feel about seeing the pronouncing of vows as a commitment to a life-journey, a process, as a trust-filled movement into possibilities, not as an accomplished fact that identifies us once and for all in a particular state of perfection that can be clearly measured?

3

Blessed Are the Poor

Solidarity with Christ's poor has for a long time now been identified as a specific way in which we as religious throughout the world are called to live out our vowed commitment. Somehow the vow of poverty and our concern for, as well as at-oneness with, God's *anawim* are seen as connected, and the persistence with which many of our community documents stress this connection marks it as undoubtedly central to our way of life in contemporary times.

The Question of Solidarity

We know that the issue of wealth and poverty is one of the most significant concerns both in the Old, as well as in the New Testament. In the Old Testament this theme comes second only to idolatry with which the oppression of the poor is often openly connected. More than five hundred verses (that is, one in every sixteen) in the New Testament are directly concerned with teachings concerning it, not to mention indirect references found in the actions of Jesus and his followers.[1] "Jesus talked more about wealth and poverty," Jim Wallis tells us, "than almost any other subject, including heaven and hell, sexual morality, the law, or violence."[2] Clearly, the poor are a central concern for Jesus and his *basileia,* and solidarity with them is a membership mandate.

In our time, however, more drastically perhaps than in any other phase in history, the cruelty of greed and self-interest is evident everywhere. Because of the advancement in media and mass communication during this century, we cannot but encounter it. Daily we receive ever more disturbing reminders of the suffering and evil brought on by a worldwide economic imbalance. The destitution of millions is its consequence.

Evil is working from ten to twelve hours a day; it is child labour, backbreaking work, the agonizing task, the workaholic obsession—all Evil. Unemployment at the same time as Butter Mountains—Himalayas of butter kept in store and going bad to the tune of millions, Everests of jam flushed down the drain, cattle killed off . . . and thrown into a common boneyard to keep prices up, the laws of free trade and the Common Market praised to high heaven (while millions die of starvation in the Sahara, in Bengal or the Horn of Africa) and extolled by people who keep our noses to the grindstone so that we can pay our taxes—those taxes with which they finance the destruction of the fruits of our labours—yes, that is what Evil is. Evil is all that is stupid, and the joyful acceptance of stupidity by those who profit by it, and by those who do not suffer because of it.[3]

We are all too familiar with statements such as this observation by Petru Dumitriu in his spiritual autobiography. They disturb us and make us feel uneasy, for we eat butter and jam and meat, and few of us go hungry. How is it, we therefore ask ourselves, that we can be in solidarity with the poor and yet eat well and live comfortably? We claim that there is for us, beyond our baptismal obligation, a vowed commitment to justice. As Gospel women and men publicly professed, we see simplicity of life and exemplary action on behalf of justice as mandatory. We simply may not indulge and live luxuriously (not even with commodities owned in common) as long as the vast majority of the world is subsisting below the level of starvation. The constitutions of my own congregation put it well: We "choose to live with less," they claim, "until all have enough." Yet the problem is that many of us live with more, much more. We live according to the life-styles of the consumer society that for many of us is our cultural model and that persuasively presents all sorts of luxuries as necessities. In America today, says John Francis Kavanaugh—and I would add, in all countries that share a similar worldview—"the compulsion to consume has become for us as deep as the exigency to survive because the Commodity Form [as opposed to the Gospel Form of living] reveals our very being and purpose as calculable solely in terms of what we possess, measurable solely by what we have and take. We *are* only insofar as we possess,"[4] and insofar as the remuneration for our work renders us capable of acquiring. This kind of cultural dogma can be very persuasive and penetrate deep—way beyond merely conscious levels of value identification and behavior. A radical questioning into the meaning of our vow of poverty, therefore, can be extremely disconcerting. With economic cruelty all around us, however, its persistence, if in the asking it truly breaks our heart, must move us to action.

The stakes are high. We are concerned here with the Gospel's central mandate on behalf of justice. As Jim Wallis puts it, our own "spiritual well-being and our relationship to the Lord are at stake."[5] All that evil requires, Dumitriu observes, is the absence of heart. "I have come to suspect," says he, "that a part of God's silence is my own; that a part of God's absence is nothing but the absence of our own hearts, of our humanity, of our friendship. . . . The absences of the human heart sometimes last a long time."[6] And that may be precisely the issue: The pain at our seeming impotence in the face of it all, and our unwilling yet, nevertheless, real participation in it, in spite of our well-meant protestations, can also prove too great. We can thus slip quite easily into a form of dualistic denial. We can profess one thing and live quite another, refusing ever to face the inconsistencies of our lives and to embrace courageously the tensions between our present cultural situation and our call as religious to live creatively toward personal and societal transformation.*

I am sure that I am not alone when I confess that I have puzzled much about why it is that so many of us appear so little moved by the radical demands of our religious profession to be for the poor (especially, it seems, when they are proclaimed and interpreted by those in our midst who, for whatever reason, see

*Many of us live in the richest parts of the world and enjoy its goods. As a professor of mine many years ago told us—a class of struggling graduate students: "Our hands are also always dirty." Sandra Schneiders explains this well in her book *New Wineskins:* "[W]e also know that we are constantly implicated in fostering the very systems that we have analyzed as unjust and exploitative. Every time we go to the bank, buy groceries, fill the gas tank, we participate in one way or another in multinational systems which are, at some near or far remove from us, exploiting the poor" (New York: Paulist Press, 1986), p. 189.

themselves as more truly representative of this Gospel mandate and wish to remind us that we should be too). To what *do* we expect to be committing ourselves when we *vow* poverty? There is, I believe, a real struggle in this question. It seems so easy to take back, one at a time, the very *things* one has given up in a moment of grace, and to find all sorts of justifications for this sad retrieval. As the musical *Nunsense* reminds us facetiously: Religious are those who "own nothing but have everything."

I have agonized, on the other hand, also over the "dos" and "don'ts" of community stipulations regarding poverty, all presented as guidelines, I know, but possessing little more than the power of prescription. I have wondered why the guidelines of community directories leave me so cold and, in themselves, fail to empower me. Why do I feel a sour taste in my mouth when I hear discussions on how much gift money may or may not be kept by a vowed religious; when I hear us complaining about signing out cars and about the luxury of those whose work allows them to have one; when the size of allowances is debated, or when I see sisters taking responsibility for monitoring what others own? In those moments it becomes clearer to me why some among us need to move out of community and monitor their own budgets. All frantic attempts at standardization strike me as hopelessly missing the point, and having little if any motivational power.

Called to Self-Sacrifice

At times of serious questioning into what poverty might mean for us today, I frequently return to Donald Nicholl's observation concerning the nature of self-sacrifice. For few, if any, religious poverty is an unavoidable affliction, a social evil to which we are bound by economic necessity. Our relation to it, therefore, needs to be one of choice, of free self-gift, of surrender. Nicholl sees self-sacrifice as "an act of *total* responsibility whereby we take complete hold of ourselves and place ourselves at the disposition of the whole; we cease to be apart and become one with the whole," and thus we " 're-present' the whole."[7] It seems to me that perhaps this is where we need to start when we reflect upon our vow.

The question arises, of course, as to when someone is capable of this kind of self-giving and what it really entails. Nicholl's vision is surprisingly vast and certainly not restricted to religious consecration. He meditates on self-giving as the leitmotif for the entire history of evolution from the first moment of creation, through the formation of the earth, to the appearance of life, the beginning of conscious life, self-awareness, and ultimately self-sacrifice in the Omega Point that is Christ.[8] With Dante he sees a connection between the outer world and the inner world of the human being, a harmony in the cosmic story. "It is the same Love," he says, "which moves our hearts as moves the sun and the other stars,"[9] as moves the amoeba and with it all subsequent forms of life, as addresses human self-awareness in all its phases of development into openness, and as ultimately brings creation to the climax of its own movement in utter self-sacrifice. In the evolutionary event nothing can be greater, says he, than the moment of Christ Jesus. In him the "new reality is the act of self-sacrifice deliberately carried out on behalf of others by a self-conscious being. Neither man [woman] nor God can go any further than that: *there is no further to go;* it is ultimate."[10]

And what of us who live in time, after the death and resurrection of Jesus? Where do we fit in the evolutionary momentum? Nicholl's answer quite simply is that because of Christ Jesus we live in the fullness of time. Because of Christ Jesus whom we have put on in baptism (and, as religious, once again through our vows) we are called as *basileia*-people to be for God's ultimate reign, a reign that is among us, but that is also not yet. Because of Christ Jesus who gave himself up, and because of the Spirit who sustains us now in this movement of self-giving, we are called into the truth of the labor pangs of creation groaning in the agony of giving birth (Eph. 1:3–10). We are called into wholeness, into holiness as the fullness of the creative process. "Holiness is not an optional extra to the process of creation but rather the whole point of it."[11]

Holiness, however, like all of creation, and this needs to be stressed, is in the process, in the birthing, in the growing, in the travail of self-emptying. It flowers in freedom, in openness, and in vision that leads to action. Holiness, therefore, is not a once-in-our-lifetime decision—not at the moment of final profession for each of us personally, nor with our general chapter decrees pronouncing the ideal for all of us collectively; not in the inscriptions and mottos on our walls, nor in the pronouncements of our directories and news letters. The Christ vision, even though it is with us in the historical now, requires our *personal appropriation* in the particular event of our individual growth into awareness and into vision. If the culminating point of evolution lies in the self-aware self-gift springing from the personal freedom and responsibility of Jesus the Christ, then living in that moment requires for each of us the same. And it is here, I believe, that we must locate our vow of poverty. No amount of chapter commitments on our behalf, valuable though they are, will make us poor; no amount of external authority will either. We may be vowed members of a congregation, and our convenant will certainly affect our way of life, but ultimately the decision to give all is ours, and this decision is the story of a lifetime of personal responsibility, of guilt, and of redemption. Religious life and corporate decisions do not absolve us from this responsibility, nor from the guilt. *We do not vow away our freedom, but assume it*—a fact sometimes ignored when in corporate pronouncements and regulations we overemphasize the collective and lose equilibrium in the tension with individual choice and responsibility.

A Personal Yes

I do not deny, of course, that as an institution, our corporate orientation on behalf of the poor is important and can be very significant. Much can be done through good stewardship, good leadership, and through the persistent yet creative anchoring of present community objectives in the charism of the founder. But a community's dreams and objectives are, in the last analysis, only as strong as its members. If their acceptance of vision statements does not ultimately spring from their own personal struggle; from their own personal journey into Christ's death and resurrection; from their own personal response to the exigencies of our time, little of lasting value and significance will come about. It is clear that we are here faced once again with the need to embrace those "deeper realities" that Rahner invited us to acknowledge, mentioned in the previous chapter: personal responsibility in the face of utter abandonment, of impotence, of being stripped even of our very self; our experiences of life, really lived fully and maturely, as it moves us into its deepest moments and asks for our total acceptance and surrender.

What if, in the light of the above discussion, we were to embrace the vow of poverty as primarily and essentially (but not by that fact only) an inner attitude, a holy disposition, toward which we come to direct ourselves in ever-more profound and sometimes agonizing movements of the heart, filling us with ever-deeper yearning even as we recognize our own personal blindness in its regard, our brokenness, and our vulnerability? What if we, in all humility, came to see this inner attitude as grace, as gift, to which we need to open ourselves, and for which we must honestly pray each day; which we can never take for granted, never measure or evaluate, not even when we work among the poorest of the poor or when we have given up every last thing we possess? What if we saw poverty as gracing us not first and foremost when we *do* anything but only when we *surrender our power?* Might it not be that then we would be moved by it to a deep solidarity with all of Christ's poor, and to authentic action on behalf of personal as well as global transformation?

Solidarity—being at one with another—is impossible unless one shares in the being of others, in their existential experience. Our stress here must be primarily on *being-with* rather than on *doing-for,* not because the latter is not important, but because the latter without the former is useless both for the receiver and for the giver. This is so precisely because, within this perspective, there still *is* a "receiver" and a "giver" and, therefore, solidarity as such has not as yet been achieved. Within a "doing-for" perspective the dualistic-hierarchical mentality of "helper-helped," be it ever so gracious, still rules our hearts. I cannot be at one with someone when I am the exclusive giver, no matter how generous the gift; no matter how hard I work. Only when I can truly let the other's need gift me; when I experience the one I "help" as giving me life, and when my services become thanksgiving, do I experience authentic solidarity, at-oneness with the poor. Then I can embrace my sisters and brothers in gratitude for needing me or for being needed by me. Then I am truly poor.[12]

Elsewhere I have meditated on the meaning of Matthew's "poverty of spirit" (Matt. 5:30), and of the virtue of poverty as primarily a blessed disposition authentically ours in direct proportion to our mature acceptance of our humanity, our personhood.[13] The reflection was in no way an attempt to sidestep the responsibility that is ours on behalf of the materially poor, but in fact intended to probe the issue of solidarity without which responsibility remains empty and cold.

The blessedness of the poor, it would seem (that which unites persons [in the true sense of that term] . . . and has them stand in solidarity with each other), is their *need* and, even more so, their *knowledge* of their need, for it is *this* that renders them open, receptive, grateful. It is this, in fact, which most authentically gives them their essential dignity as persons (from Latin *per*, "through," and *sonare*, "sound"): those who are open enough and empty enough, in need enough to receive and to give forth (return to the giver) what they have received, through gratitude. A "person" is one *through whom* the sound of creative love can flow, one who can receive and respond in the utter vulnerability of releasement. As such, s/he is blessed in a very basic sense; s/he is poor.[14]

It is clear that what we are touching on belongs to the depth dimension of the human personality. Economic advantage or disadvantage is, as it were, only secondary—not in time so much as in essence—to this primary poverty that constitutes us in our being and that, if recognized and accepted, holds us in solidarity with all of humankind. The invitation to *become who we are,* to which authentic Gospel living calls us every day, is a call to recognition—to full consciousness of self as poor. It is a call to self-emptying, a stripping of all power fixations, roles, false symbols of prestige. It is a plea to surrender to all the pain that this implies, in order to be born into wholeness, into the fullness of time into which Christ Jesus redeemed us. It is an offer to replace our "hearts of stone" with "hearts of flesh"—a call to softness of heart. This, I believe, is the first and the most essential mandate of our vow. It does not separate us from other Christians, for they too, through the Gospel, are called to this

poverty. It claims us, however, by our specific allegiance to it on
the day of our profession. Through our membership in a religious congregation we highlight this Gospel mandate and we
surrender to it publicly. The resulting responsibility ought not to
be underestimated. Poverty is from God in Christ Jesus who
"emptied himself" to become one of us (Phil. 2:7). When we
vow poverty we vow *movement into God;* we vow to allow ourselves to be changed, to be freed from ego-enhancement and
control, and to be faced with the mystery of our own wounded-
ness and sinfulness which, in turn, will enable us to encounter
others as our sisters and brothers, and to commit ourselves with
integrity to justice.

True Poverty

I believe that I am truly poor and, therefore, blessed—energized and empowered by God—only when I can radically stand
in my own vulnerability and weakness and proclaim the goodness of God who "fills the hungry with good things and sends
the rich away empty" (Luke 1:53), not because God does not
want to give them anything but because they are too full to notice any insufficiency. They need to be emptied out first before
they can even see the dynamics of holiness and justice.

An interesting little story from the East illustrates this Mag-
nificat truth in beautiful simplicity: It is said that the god Shiva
decided one day to take on the form of a wise and holy person
and to visit humankind. The news of his presence spread quickly
and holy people from everywhere came to him to get an esti-
mate on their chances for salvation. They cited all their achievements and praiseworthy deeds in the hope of being rewarded
with salvation as soon as possible. Being generally convinced of
their good works, they were usually disappointed when Shiva
cited the number of reincarnations that would still be necessary
for them to achieve eternal union with him. To one person he
gave three, to another seven, and so on. Very last among the
long line of seekers was a tiny little man truly ashamed of the
insignificance of his life and aware of his many sins. All he had
to say for himself was that he loved creation and tried not to

hurt anyone. He simply hoped for the promise that some day salvation would be his for he loved God dearly in spite of the poverty of his achievements. When Shiva, after some hesitation, awarded him one thousand more reincarnations, the man danced for joy and gratitude. It is said that suddenly this man turned into a flame. The energy of his enthusiasm (Greek, *en*, "in," *theos*, "god") and his humble recognition of all as grace had transformed him. Shiva too became pure light. The flames united and moved into eternal bliss.[15] In our own tradition this story brings to mind the parable of the Pharisee and the Publican (Luke 18:10–14). The latter, in the recognition of his need for mercy, went home justified. It is not primarily what we do, but the surrender of our love even as we recognize our own poverty, that blesses us.

I believe that I am poor and can, therefore, be hospitable when I know in the very core of my being that everything I have is gift. I believe that I am poor when I can embrace my own darkness as truly mine, and yet know that I am loved; when I can experience the power of compassion within me and through me, because I have known the dregs of the passion and have stood in it and been embraced by God. I believe that I am truly poor when that compassion transforms my world and the needs I experience in it for myself; when it allows me to see the nothingness in all things and leads me to authentic hunger for justice and for God; when it directs and motivates my actions and radically moves me to embrace others in their poverty.

The Unity of Interiority and Justice

It is becoming ever clearer to me as I reflect more deeply upon the seeming inconsistencies between what some of us as religious profess and subsequently do, that the vow of poverty, as well as simplicity, hospitality, and compassion, which are its fruit, will not survive without depth vision. This view is not, of course, shared by all. The dualism of our upbringing can split our world in both directions. In this way, however, holiness and justice will never meet. For the pietist of the "old days," the worry about perfection leaves compassion to those whose designated ministry it is: the missionary, the minister in the "inner city," workers in soup kitchens and shelters for the homeless. But activists of today can also fall victim to this dichotomy. "Concentration on human interiority," in the words of Ann Belford Ulanov, "seems to them inevitably to bring with it neglect of the real problems of our time: the social, the political, and the cultural."[16] Concern for personal development, contemplation, and the whole quest for the holy can, by this manner of thinking, be quite easily dismissed as an ivory tower luxury; as navel gazing. "My work is my prayer," they say, and fail to recognize the power of religious aspiration as the backdrop and underpinning of all authentic and truly effective work on behalf of justice. Thus they deprive themselves of its passion and their works of true compassion.

Personal growth and social concerns are not mutually exclusive, nor should the relationship between them be understood as merely sequential: "once I get my own act together, I will help others," or "once all my work for justice is done, I will worry about my own development—go on an extended retreat, pray." The justice of Jesus was held within his holiness and, as Ulanov points out, "some of the greatest advocates of the contemplative life did more to move society in the direction of social justice than the most ardent social reformers." Activists, she claims, often fail to see how "fundamental to social disorder is the disorder within each of us and how much a re-ordering of society depends upon a re-ordering of individual lives."[17] The story of Kiaochau comes to mind. Works of justice can also suffer from the drought mentality.

To be in solidarity with the poor is to stand in the truth of the human condition and to know that I am a part. This takes self-knowledge and humble self-acceptance. No social justice theory, no moral philosophy, no fixed doctrine, contains within itself the answer to the injustices of this world; only the human heart softened by grace. Holistic spirituality is the journey toward a soft heart. When I experience in the very core of my being those who bleed as shedding my blood; those who hunger as aching with my pain; those who sin as performing my deeds; when I truly encounter the gift that is the human community even in its darkest moments and, deeper still, know myself to hold that darkness as well, then I am at one with humankind groaning for the fullness of creation, the fullness of our redemption in Christ.

The insight described here, however, does not come easily. For it even the most sincere among us need to be "stripped," to be "seared," to experience the desolation and loneliness and defeat that makes it possible for us to acknowledge and see our own fundamental emptiness and need, and to recognize this as our glory. We also need the silence, the space, the inwardness to acknowledge that the stripping constitutes our journey into God; that it is a process that ultimately returns us to the poverty that we are; that it is essential for the experience of Christian companioning and solidarity; that it is the stuff our vow is made of. Nor should this discourage any of us, for whether we realize it or not, we are held in this process already. It belongs to the birth pangs of creation in Christ. Ours is merely the task of conscientization, of acceptance, and of holding it within ourselves toward personal and communal Christification.

To go deep within the life of our own psyche really unites us with every other psyche. To touch the deep unconscious dimensions of our own personal problems introduces us to that level of association that is really communal. . . . At this level our own particular problems come to serve as entries into collective human problems: we may even see that our own small solutions contribute a great deal to the ongoing human struggle with these problems. . . . We recognize as inevitable the connection between self and other, and come to see that our most deeply personal experiences are inextricable from participation in the human community. As Lady Julian of Norwich says, we are knit into the substance of God, hence we feel knit into one another at the deepest level.[18]

Clearly what we experience here is compassion—a passionate being with the other in his or her passion because we have been there, we are there, we hold it in the depths of our own heart. Ulanov sees "transparency" as a symbolic representation of this kind of compassion. The division between social issues and personal concerns turns out to be illusory, for there is a shining through: "At the most intimate depths of the soul, we see reaching through the communal, and from the farthest reaches of the communal, the deeply personal textures of our own being and of the other's being."[19]

Toward Softness of Heart

In Jungian terms what we have meditated on is called the process of individuation. Whitmont describes it as "always a road, a way, a process, travel or travail, a dynamism; it is never, at least not while one lives in time and space, a static or accomplished state."[20] Much of it fits into the second journey of our life when ego building gives way to the encounter with deeper realities of the self. The call to holiness, of course, is not denied to anyone, but the movement from an idealistic to a realistic perspective on life happens generally in the second half of our sojourn here on earth. It is its bitter sweetness, its deprivation, its poverty that we are here dealing with.

I find it interesting that today, within our societal context, when and where meditations such as the above have (because of depth psychology and a revived interest in mystical thought and holistic living) finally become possible, a much larger proportion of the newer members of religious congregations are in, or at least close to, the second journey of life. It is as if, consciously or not, they are involved with these concerns and see religious life as an opportunity to address them. I believe we need to meet them there. The poverty we vow and invite them to join us in is a commitment to open ourselves up to a softening of the heart. In this commitment all works on behalf of justice and mercy are guided and supported by a fundamental disposition of at-oneness with the human family. This supplies them with the energy of compassion and solidarity that they need but that for all of us requires a lifelong process of self-emptying. We cannot invite or plan this process. It befalls us. Our vow is our willingness, our trust—our surrender to, and our dwelling in gratitude for, the vision that this process opens up for us: a vision that we know is grace, laced with pain though it may be.

It is my conviction that when we vow poverty we commit ourselves to nothing less than the depth of the Gospel as the Christ event unfolds in us each day anew. Authentic actions flow from this event and, because of it, will be primarily self-motivated and self-energized. Our constitutions, reflections on our lived experience and interpreted at all times out of that existential situation and the societal context of the moment, need, given the above reflection, to be understood not so much as rules, therefore, but as vision statements, love statements, for mutual empowerment.

Some Reflections on Our Existential Situation

At this point it may be necessary for us to pause in this meditation and look more specifically for the concrete, for some of the practical situations and decisions regarding poverty that address us in our everyday life. We may want to contextualize what we have reflected upon into our lived reality, asking ourselves how empowerment takes shape or how it is prevented in our daily lives.*

Clearly, with respect to living the vow of poverty, our discussion has ruled out the element of prescriptive or regulative goal setting extraneous to the membership. Sandra Schneiders says it well when she points out that "little is to be gained and much lost by attempts to standardize the practice of poverty."[21] This is particularly true in large, sometimes multinational congregations where diversity of life-style and ministry is a given and the relativity of the notion of "poverty" becomes especially clear. Furthermore, on the more individual level, whether we like to admit this or not, our experience (especially of the last twenty or more years since Vatican II and the emergence of the adult religious) has demonstrated that we can write whatever we want into our directories or constitutions, we can extrapolate forever at our community meetings and even call it discernment. If, however, the insight and subsequent experience of our own inner poverty has not graced us and called us forth, our words will be empty and our actions without energy. Poverty, quite simply, is not primarily something we say or do or practice. It is first and foremost something we *are* and *are becoming*. The tension in which we are held here is precisely between our convenantal at-oneness in community, on the one hand, and our commitment

---

*The examples and suggestions offered here are by no means exhaustive; nor do I wish to imply that the interpretations given here are the only valid ones. I offer them with the same intentions as for the preceding: as "gathering-in" material for reflections that I hope will lead us and our congregations more deeply into a holistic spirituality, into wholeness.

to maturation as individuals, on the other. The very concepts of covenant and community depend on maturity. One assumes the other.

Maturity, however, simply does not happen when adults are kept at dependency status, nor does authentic community. It is "institution" instead, and displays all the regressive characteristics that belong to this kind of setting. The problem for us, of course, is that too many of us endured precisely that kind of setting for too long. We were "formed" in it from the earliest moments of our commitment, and in this "formation" we were given all the answers; answers to questions we had not even asked and, therefore, often did not know what to do with. We certainly received the answers to poverty and how, step by step, it was to be lived. With this the process of emergence—the movement into personal insight and appropriation—was frequently stifled. We became dependent instead and this dependency was hailed as humility. The entire process was, to a large extent, external to us—imposed from the outside and accepted blindly. Most things were accessible through permission, and discernment as to their relevance in one's life was left to the (assumed) wisdom—believed to be bestowed with the "grace of state"—of the superior.

After Vatican II it seemed that things drastically changed. The word was "experimentation" and religious all over the country were sent out to study and learn to think on their own. We attended workshops of every type. The concern seemed to be to move us as quickly as possible from preadolescent dependency to the interdependent perspective that, given our chronological age, was expected of us. Emotionally some of us even succeeded, after a relatively brief span of retrieving lost adolescent time. I do not believe, however, that the structures of our institutions ever gave way enough to the need for the adequate economic independence that precedes any mature ability to share. No one can freely give what she or he has never had. No one can freely share when the sharing is dictated extraneously. The assumption that because we vowed something we willed it simply does not hold up when one considers that what most of us vowed to do without we had not yet experienced.

That one cannot be interdependent without first having moved through independence is a psychological given. The movement through independence will take its own time and will have to be taken seriously if poverty is to be understood holistically. Perhaps the notion of religious life as a life-style more specifically for men and women in the second half of life's journey (or at least after independence has been adequately developed and has moved to interdependence) needs to be explored and taken more seriously. What is certain, however, is that the entering of mature persons (by this I mean individuals *aware* of the journey they are on and willing and able to grow) needs to be encouraged. At the same time, our own growth into maturity is an ongoing concern and the institutional structures that surround it need to be seriously and critically rethought lest those who join us regress, losing the freedom that has brought them, and we never acquire it.

"Haves" and "Have-Nots"

A member of the leadership team in my own community asked me not long ago whether I agreed with the statement that community life is divided between the "haves" and the "have-nots." This initially is quite a shocking statement for those of us who still live in the myth of "communal" or "standardized" poverty in which we were "formed." It is an uncomfortable question, to be true, but is it not worth reflection?

To begin with, the life-style of the various communities in any congregation certainly varies considerably. What some consider a necessity, others, in their understanding of what comprises a simple life-style, have come to see as luxury; yet members of either group profess the same vow. Nor is it necessarily productive or advisable for the provincial superior on the yearly visit to point out inconsistencies and demand change, for even if external compliance does follow, what about the change of heart? Are those who hanker after what is not theirs truly poor? I am not suggesting that blatant luxuries or the "hamster mentality"—acquisitiveness: the indiscriminate collecting of anything and everything one can lay one's hands on—should not be challenged. I am merely pointing out that compliance remains immature unless there is a change of heart and an inner honesty that distinguishes needs from desire.

Our individual life-styles also show great variance. I do not think that I exaggerate when I say that if any of us truly want something badly enough, we can usually figure out a way to get it, if not through the community, either officially or unofficially for our use, then through our parents or family, or through our friends. Some of us have the fringe benefits of our office—we have credit cards—and, depending on our interpretation, use them to "ease the burden" of our congregational responsibilities. Some of us travel a great deal and need the wardrobe of professional life; others do not. Some of us have no family at all and stay home—sometimes alone—on holidays and feasts. Some of us live alone and manage our own budgets; others live in the motherhouse and never have a chance to plan even a menu.

The issue of haves and have-nots, in whatever way one wants to look at it, undoubtedly exists in community life and, when lack of compassion or selfishness is its cause, cannot be ignored. Often, however, the reason for it is simply that the diverse values toward which the vow of poverty directs us cannot always be obtained by uniform practices in its observance: "Our exercise of hospitality in certain circumstances may conflict with our desire to eliminate certain types of food or drink from our diet for ascetical reasons," for example, or "our effective participation in certain political actions for the sake of justice may involve expenditures we would rather not make."[22] The complexity of our ministerial and communal involvements today makes standardization simply obsolete and cumbersome. Our concern here, therefore, is not so much that the issue of haves and have-nots exists in community, but rather that it is an issue and why.

A student of mine one time described her interpretation of the vow of poverty as placing emphasis not on whether we have or do not have things, but on whether *things have us*. She had struggled for a long time, she told me, observing "religious affluence," until this interpretation came to her. Heidegger speaks of the attitude she described as *releasement:* letting things "enter our daily life, and at the same time leav[ing] them outside, that is, let[ting] them alone, as things which are nothing absolute but remain dependent upon something higher."[23] We are here, once again, in the realm of disposition, of that poverty of spirit that I discussed at the beginning of this chapter and that alone gives energy to an authentic letting-go and letting-be.

Conformity in possessions is, I believe, a thing of the past and, whether it ever was a fact or not, I do not believe we need to mourn it, for I doubt that it was either realistic or healthy to begin with. Releasement, as Heidegger describes poverty of spirit, is rarely if ever achieved through conformity in this manner. It is achieved through a gradual letting go, and through vision obtained in the slow process of life. It is grace. When I hanker after Sister K's computer, I am no poorer than she. When I can let her have it and rejoice in her use of it, I am as rich as she. It is of little value if I sit in shocked silence in front of the community television alone, while my brothers watch their favorite show in their own rooms, each owning a private set. What might benefit us all, however, is to explore the reasons why they need to isolate themselves so. Perhaps in some situations we will need to direct our attention, rather, to the one who dominates the community television for, it seems to me, that he or she violates not only community life, but may also need to question his or her sense of poverty. This person *possesses* what we all own.

And what of personal budgets? Some of us have very small ones by choice or by guilt, others have considerably larger ones. Some of us get money from home; others get things bought for them instead. Still others have their family and friends pay for every dinner out and even for vacations. "We are religious," some of us will claim, and look to our community or to others to supply our needs. I believe that the problem here lies not primarily in how much we get or keep, but that we consider consistent "getting" at all as a viable adult way of living. This kind of "poverty" can be an excuse for not growing up. It can also be the reason for once more regressing.

An example of this form of regression taken from society at large can be found in the consequences of what has come to be called "momism" in the American family today. In what might now be regarded as a classic work of contemporary social psy-

chology Hendrik M. Ruitenbeek speaks of the decline in the
American male's security and maturity, and of a general male
regression as caused by this phenomenon. To describe it he
quotes Robert Odenwald's reference to a five-year-old's observation that "daddies pay the bills in restaurants but . . . mothers
give them the money beforehand."[24] By the laws of "momism,"
daddies earn the salary, but mothers give them their allowance
and supply anything over and above, only to keep the image of
adulthood up. Daddies in fact, however, are treated like the oldest dependents. We are not here concerned with the whys of
"momism" in our age, nor with its validity (in many ways it has
already been supplanted by the much more complex phenomenon of a two-salary family). We are looking rather at its seeming
similarity to the "getting" mentality of "holy" dependency for
men and women alike. Both cases, I believe, either prevent maturation in the first place, or encourage an inappropriate return
to childishness later. Neither of them foster the acceptance of
personal monetary responsibility or the development of concern
for others. When one's needs (imagined or real) are taken care of
without any significant personal investment, one cannot expect
to mature. It is true, of course, as Sandra Schneiders points out,
that contemporary religious "are participating more directly and
extensively in the handling of the finances of their local communities and institutes and assuming increasing responsibility for
the ordinary economic affairs of their own lives."[25] These are
certainly steps in the right direction. Rare still, however, is the
religious even today who in her daily choices will truly be personally affected by this participation in community finances.
The growth in awareness here seems slow. And, whereas I do
not wish to minimize the importance of what we are doing, I
for one have not as yet seen it shift us to any large extent toward
an authentic personal and mature sense of fiscal responsibility.
We are as a whole carefree and taken care of, and, as pleasant as
this may be, it simply is not real.

I am not out to propose a solution to our dilemma here. It is
serious, and needs more heads and hearts than mine. I do not
believe, however, that hiding behind canon law as intransigent
and as opposed to any change in the way we distribute and han-
dle money can save us much longer from having to deal with

this matter. Institutional compliance to age-old paradigms of church law may perhaps still work for us collectively. Thus, as institutes we can even now, with relative success, be "for the poor" and share community wealth with the oppressed. The money we may spend as institutes before we need canonical approval is sizeable. We can also mission those among us who feel called to work for justice near and far, and we can send them in our name and with our support. Laudable though this may be, it can nevertheless dull our individual consciences. When the institute does this, I can easily take the credit, which costs me nothing. If, however, we are to deal with growth into personal responsibility for justice and, therefore, a personal appropriation of the vow of poverty by each one among us, we need to address maturity issues and foster the natural human development pattern from dependence through independence to interdependence. Here church law (which generally disregards, if it is at all aware of, the findings of developmental and social psychology) will be of little help, if not an actual hindrance, to us. Efforts in this area will require tremendous creativity and daring—nothing short of visionaries, who can risk the challenge of thinking into tradition and coupling this with contemporary insight and learning—to bring about transformation. Of course, we always need to balance individual development with larger congregational concerns, but we cannot ignore it. Certain communities of non-canonical status have tried this, I am told, with some surprising (even financial) success. Members in some instances manage their own salaries and give what they can to the common account. Their sacrifice, I have heard, is often considerable.

Contrary to what our "formation" may have led us to believe, there is no divinely decreed, foolproof model for the vow of poverty. There is only the mandate to compassionate presence, to sharing, to being for others out of our wealth and our want. The risks of rethinking the way we live out our vow of poverty are high. Ultimately, of course, we do not "live out" or vow anyway, nor do we "practice" it. We rather commit ourselves to live into its grace and to learn from it daily. One can always worry about abuses and in any movement toward responsible freedom there will be abuses, but we can hardly deny that we are free of them now. In the last analysis, our mandate is to foster growth into wholeness; growth toward maturity experienced in community. Holiness as such cannot be ascribed to an institute but only to its members. Whatever fosters it in them will augment the larger congregation and ultimately bring justice to the whole church.

Questions for Focus, Reflection, Discussion

1. Have you experienced the pain of your powerlessness in the face of economic injustice in the world? Can you cite an example? How do you react to the statement that there is for us, nevertheless, an unwilling yet real participation in this injustice, that "our hands are also always dirty"?

2. How can you see self-sacrifice as an authentic expression of your vow of poverty? "We may be vowed members of a congregation, and our convenant will certainly affect our way of life, but ultimately the decision to give all is ours, and this decision is the story of a lifetime of personal responsibility, of guilt, and of redemption." What is your reaction to this statement?

3. "Only when I can truly let the other's need gift me; when I experience the one I 'help' as giving me life, and when my service becomes thanksgiving, do I experience authentic solidarity, at-oneness with the poor." Have you experienced this insight? What does it mean to you?

4. How, in your view, can works of justice suffer from the "drought mentality" described at the beginning of chapter 1?

5. Could piety without concern for justice become insipid pietism? Might this be a danger for Christian churches, for religious congregations, for religious?

6. How, in your own experience as a religious, have you seen yourself moving from dependence, to independence, to interdependence? Can you cite specific examples to validate your experience? Do you see a need to address this issue further? What does interdependence mean to you now?

7. How has the "haves" and "have-nots" issue in religious life affected you? What is your reaction? Do you see "releasement" as a fitting response here?

8. Have you experienced the "getting" mentality of immature dependency? How can we as religious foster individual fiscal responsibility?

4

Community for Mission

In the preceding chapters I have been primarily concerned with introducing religious vows generally and the vow of poverty in particular within the context of holistic spirituality. I have tried to move away from the dualism of our past and to ask how our way of living into our baptismal promises might help us reach wholeness, maturity, and integrity. The intention of these pages has been to approach the vows as our way of living in the fullness of time; as our way of moving ever more deeply into the Christ event. For this reason I proposed that they be understood not primarily in a prescriptive sense—telling us what we must do and what we may not do—but rather in an attitudinal sense: opening us up to a disposition in which we stand and are held, so to speak, and into which commit ourselves to grow in ever greater longing for holiness and for wholeness. I suggested that what we vow is open-ended, a process, not a final product at any given or determinable moment. It is a commitment to a depth that takes hold of us ever more fully as we move into our identity as religious.

The present chapter will concern itself with our vowed life in relation to community. My emphasis will be specifically on consecrated celibacy, on encountering life—all of life—out of a celibate identity.[1] It is my conviction that this vow especially speaks to our living in community, and I believe that unless we realize what community can no longer be and what authentic community might be for us today, talk about celibacy will be wasted. The opposite, I think, is true also: Unless we embrace the depth meaning of consecrated celibacy, our communities will wither away, atrophy and collapse.

Our Emphasis on Mission

Since Vatican II the mandate to foster "community for mission" has been given much reflection, action, and energy among us. Holistically speaking this might mean that we have steadily been moving toward internalizing and celebrating in our midst the multifaceted breakthrough of God in the world, and that we have attempted to do this particularly by witnessing to God's compassion in many different ways. Diversification of ministries in most religious communities especially in the United States has flourished and, although many congregations may still identify themselves in broad terms by the apostolate of their founders (be it education, health care, social work, etc.), their understanding of these ministries in most cases has remarkably expanded, if not always in expressed theory, most definitely in praxis. It has, for example, become clear to many of us that education can take place in many different ways and that for the true educator the world is the classroom. Today we educate as always when we teach in public, diocesan, or private schools, in colleges and universities, but we know that we also do so when we minister to the sick and the dying and share with them the word of God by our presence and love, or when we rally people on behalf of justice, make music, paint; when we give spiritual direction; when we counsel and facilitate and organize retreat programs. In the area of health care, as well, we accept today that sickness is not only of the body or of the mind but can be a social phenomenon, and that healing, therefore, transcends the hospital. We work for it also when we counsel those broken in spirit or in heart; when we inspire the depressed, challenge an oppressive system, provide and build houses for the destitute, work to resolve conflictual situations and facilitate dialogue. Ministries of every kind abound in most present-day religious congregations. It seems that we have realized and accepted that our primary vocation is to service where there is the greatest need, and that our commonality lies not so much in the *what* of our ministry as in the *how*, in the *why*, and in the *end*.

Not only did we expand our ministries in the years since Vatican II, we also have become educated in so doing. This is particularly true for women religious who today count among the most educated women in the United States. We took seriously the call to service in contemporary society. Having returned to the charism of those who founded our congregations, we noted our inadequacy vis-à-vis a world of intellectual as well as practical sophistication. We knew that to be sisters and brothers to the modern man and woman and thus truly to be of service to the church in the modern world, we needed to stand within it, to be educated at the best schools, to minister responsibly and viably as women and men with a contemporary perspective and contemporary faith response. We knew that witnessing does not take place in seclusion or out of an ivory tower mentality; that wholeness, healing, and holiness in this world is achieved when the Christ event can be witnessed in the ordinary, and when every man, woman, and child in any situation, under any condition, can proclaim the Gospel as their own. And so we knew why we needed to diversify our ministries. As our numbers grew smaller we diversified even more. We came to live into, and hopefully trust, the power of the "mustard seed" and of the "leaven in the dough." We proclaimed "church" and we took ownership of "church."

For the active religious, especially in America today, "church" and, within "church," *mission,* is an all-inclusive term, a holistic concept. Our obedience as public witnesses to the reign of God in this world is a *standing in a listening posture* vis-à-vis its needs as they unfold among us. We recognize today more than ever before—precisely because of our journey since Vatican II—that the *eschaton* is here. The Christ event in all its depth, its pain, and its glory is ours to proclaim by our public presence. For the contemporary religious this means reverence for and commitment to the empowerment of God's people everywhere. We have worked hard at educating ourselves and developing our ministries to this end. Religious without doubt and without the least exaggeration are among the most efficient and well-trained ministers in today's church. We are good at what we do and our recognition of this should give us cause for celebration.

But we are also tired, overextended, and overworked, discouraged at times and angry. The enthusiasm among us is all too often burning at a low flicker and many among us are wondering what has gone wrong. It is obvious, I think, that especially for women religious the climate within the official church has in many instances been anything but inviting. The struggle that many of us experienced in seeking approval for our constitutions, and the persistent inconsistencies we encounter between the church's teachings in the area of justice and its actual practice* are enough to anger and fatigue even the most loyal among us—and perhaps especially them. It is not my intention here to address these issues. Others more qualified than I can do so more effectively. I mention them merely for the sake of completeness and to prevent my reflections on the reasons for disease and discouragement among religious today from appearing simplistic or one-sided. As was explored in chapter 1, we live in complex times. There are, therefore, usually many and varied reasons for any single phenomenon. They cannot always be dealt with at the same time. It is a fact that religious who minister in the church today are often exhausted and discouraged. The ecclesial climate certainly must take its share of the blame for this.

The Neglected Piece

Another reason for discouragement, however, and the one I wish to reflect on, is community life itself. It is my impression, and dialogue with other religious seems to confirm, that it has been the neglected piece, the stepchild, if you will, of renewal since Vatican II. It may be that the energy we spent on ministerial training left us precious little for community reform, so that the thoughtful development of a life-style suited to the educated adults we had become has lagged far behind—if, in fact, it has been able to move at all. Often when I hear reference to religious life as "community for mission" (i.e., "*we have* community *to empower us* for mission"), I want to ask what has happened to the "community" part of the equation. And, once again, I wonder whether the "doing" dimension of life (ministry) has not been overstressed at the expense of the "being" dimension.

Even today we still seem to spend endless meetings (and, therefore, all possible spare energy available to us after hard

*The issues of women's rights and of just wages for church employees are cases in point.

hours of ministry) writing mission statements and identifying apostolic priorities for our congregations or our various provinces. Somehow, it would appear, we feel the need in all this diversity to be clear about what we do and to identify our at-oneness there. We hope thus, among other things, to present a unity to ourselves, to the church, and to the world that may also, we think, draw new members once again and give us direction: the corporate identity we lost when we ceased functioning collectively in our schools and hospitals. We come together to discuss and define what we do and why we do it, hoping somehow, I think, to experience companionship that way. Valuable though this is, however, the fact that at-oneness is primarily a matter of being and only because of this can be experienced in doing seems to escape many of us. As a consequence community priorities get translated into exclusively apostolic terms and how we live together, meet, reach out to, and experience each other rarely gets any reflection time (simply because there is none left over) though these questions cry out for answers deep in the heart of each one of us.

In order to *do* with authenticity one first has to *be*. By this I mean that one has to dwell in one's own integrity and be empowered there. For this, I believe, wholesome, healthy, and intentional community is essential. The question that cries out to us for answers, therefore, concerns the meaning of community for us. What kind of community do we need? How can our being together empower us and enhance our various ministries? One of the major reasons, I think, why the issue of a healthy rethinking and intentional revisioning of community life has so long been neglected in our renewal process is precisely our tendency to draw too tight a connection between community and mission; to establish, in other words, an exclusive one-way relationship.

Although it is true that an empowering community is certainly important for the minister, to assume that the sole purpose of community is to enhance our ministries reduces community to a means toward action and neglects to see it in its own nature; in its being dimension, as I refer to it. This often has the unfortunate consequence of our addressing community solely in terms of how it can adjust itself to further mission.

Thus we experience community life more like a "bed and break-fast" place, as Mary Wolff-Salin calls it,[2] and we bring about the exact opposite of what we hope for. A house to which I am assigned or to which I move simply because it is advantageous to my ministry because of space, location, traveling needs, is precisely that—a convenient place. It may, however, have little to do with community, and unless other issues—issues that belong to *being* a community—are also discerned, I cannot expect them automatically to happen. A convenient place does not guarantee that there is anyone at all in the house "with whom [I] have anything in common, whether by age, training, interest, or personality."[3] How can I, therefore, expect to experience empowerment in such a situation?

Means are always evaluated in terms of their appropriateness to their end. If ministry alone is our end and looms as exclusively important, community will be seen, consciously or not, only in terms of adjusting to mission. But we are *persons* in mission, not mere functionaries. As persons we have needs that may differ from our needs as workers. Marx may believe that if our work fulfills us we are fulfilled, but we as Christians know that even Jesus went apart to be with his community and his friends; that he chose his companions and cared for their well-being as persons. He also rested and relaxed, and asked his disciples to do the same. Our living together today presents us with pressing concerns: "Have members [of a religious community] any obligation to each other at all," for example, "or are all their obligations outside? Is contemporary religious life, notably active, a wholly individualistic situation? . . . In other words, if I do my assigned job, is my daily life wholly my concern?"[4] Is the apostolate all that matters? These are questions, I believe, that need to be faced, if we dare look seriously at some of the reasons for our exhaustion and disenchantment with our life-style.

Our spirituality, our charism, is deeper than common apostolic priorities, important though these are. Community is more than a means. It is my conviction that to live in community is, in fact, an essential dimension of religious life as a whole; that one is *called* to live in community, as others are called to live a true marriage.[5] This may not always mean physical proximity or "life in common," but it does mean that those who share this bonding are also those committed in a special way to furthering and empowering individuation in each other. This is neither easy nor painless. Mary Wolff-Salin claims that "for the religious, the struggles of life with both God and community . . . suppl[y] the raw materials and the 'obstacles to conquer' for this growth process."[6] It is dealt with too superficially if ministry is seen as its only forum, and too arrogantly or naively if it is assumed as completed by the minister no matter how old he or she is or how experienced. Maturity or individuation is a process that enfolds us and challenges us throughout our life. It is "as essential a part of human motivation as hunger, thirst, aggression, sexuality, and pressures toward finding relaxation and attaining happiness."[7] Community (for the religious called to it and living in it) is a powerful help toward realizing and furthering this individuation.

What about Community?

What, then, of the first part of our motto: "community for mission"? How would things have to be? Without in any way presuming to offer a complete response, I suggest the following merely as my part of what I believe needs to be an ongoing discernment of tremendous significance for the turning point in contemporary religious life. It is my conviction that a community in which each one of us can dwell in his or her own integrity will, first and foremost, have to be a community not only of women/men, but also *for* women/men *as* women/men, that is, a community of adults *for* adults *as* adults. Sandra Schneiders, I believe, helps clarify this observation by making an appropriate distinction between community styles as lived in what she calls "primary family" and "secondary family" settings.[8] The "primary family" is the community of one's birth. It provides father and mother and often sisters and brothers. In it one is a child related to parents (and other children). The "secondary family" one chooses. In it, as spouses, for example, one is presumed to be an adult. In the primary model of community most members function as children most of the time—they are led and it is presumed that at least initially decisions have to be made for them by competent authority.

It is clear that this model is not foreign to any of us, not only because we all have had parents, we all were children once upon a time, but also because many of us have lived in religious community before Vatican II. It is also, I believe, clear that this model no longer works for us as contemporary, educated women and men in diverse ministries. Sandra Schneiders puts it well:

Since all the members of a religious community are at least chronologically adults and ideally psychological and spiritual adults as well, it is counter-productive if not destructive for them to play the role of children at home while trying to function as adults in all other arenas of their lives. This play-acting leads to infantilism, psychological regression, alienation of responsibility, guilt, and malformation of conscience among other things. The appropriate relationship between members of a community, whatever their role in the group, is that of adult to adult. Whatever else it might be, the religious community is not a two-generation family and the primary family model is radically inadequate.

Having laid aside the primary family as model for religious community living we face the problem of finding another model which is more adequate. My suggestion is that the appropriate model is that of *a community of friends who are co-disciples in ministry.*[9]

A similar suggestion was made a few years earlier by Joan Chittister when, "futurizing" about religious life and the disappearance of large institutions, she observed: "This will affect lifestyle as well as ministry, relationships, as well as work. *Friendship communities rather than work communities* will be more likely to form." Putting her finger right on the polarities of community and work that we have been discussing, she follows this observation by an interesting and certainly hope-filled projection concerning spirituality: "Communal rather than individual spirituality may likely find more emphasis as well, when groups discover that since they do not form around common works anymore, they must form around something of more sustaining value than simply a common philosophy."[10] The struggle in present-day community life is, of course, precisely around these issues but I do not see that we as a whole have discovered our gathering priorities as yet. It is my hope that what Joan Chittister projected in 1983 is in process, however. The crisis in which community life finds itself today may be a sign of this,

and a holistic spirituality that empowers those held together in
bonds of friendship and mutual support would certainly do
much for authentic renewal here.

But what of the "friendship communities" she anticipates?
What kind of friendship is it that fosters community and co-
discipleship in ministry? What kind of bonding ought to happen
or might be hoped for in our communities if we *as* women and
men, as adults in truly mature ways, are to empower each other
to minister for the Gospel? I believe that a deeper understanding
and living of our vow of celibacy can be of great significance as
we attempt to respond to these questions.

Celibacy as the Vow of Community

What has fascinated me in reading many of our new constitutions during the last several years is the stress we seem to be
placing on *communal loving* and *being loved* in our description of
what this vow means to us. It seems to me that something original is happening here: a vision, not new of course—Benedict
had it way back when[11]—but original for our time, and after
many years of drought.

More often than not in our ecclesial tradition consecrated celibacy has been interpreted in terms of "giving up." Thus, the
decisions not to marry, not to engage in genital love, not to have
children and enjoy family, fatherhood, or motherhood (always,
of course, made toward a greater end) were all primary in the
identification of this vow. Books supplementing our study of it
usually went into dualistic-hierarchical details about its excellence; its connection with various stages of human love, with
purity, with chastity; its purpose and end; its levels of renuncia-
tion; its uses and abuses.[12] To be sure, the asceticism demanded
by the vow is not ignored in our documents today, even if it is
often only indirectly mentioned (by reference to apostolic motivations, for example). What is of interest, however, is the primacy that such concepts as "mutual love," "friendship," and
"support for one another" receive in today's constitutions. We
all know that these modes of relationship also have their sacri-
ficial dimension, but in this context it does not lend itself easily
to analysis, to dissection, and is met in "living" rather than

in "listing." It is, at best, described; never clearly defined. There seems to be a natural invitation, therefore, in our documents to embrace "deeper realities," what Rahner calls the "transcendental"[13]—the "mystery" rather than the measurable, the categorical. Perhaps, then, we need to ask into this depth, and wonder what it means for us to "love as consecrated celibates." To what *do* we commit ourselves when we take this vow, and what significance does it have communally?

In a lecture I gave on this topic to a group of women religious in the Midwest not too long ago, I suggested that the living of consecrated celibacy for me means *immersing myself into the pain (as well as the joy) of life fully lived.* "I believe that when I promise consecrated celibacy," I told these women, "I promise to journey into the agony and the ecstasy of relationship; into the turmoil, the pain, the revelation of myself to myself, of others and of God which loving nonpossessively will open up for me.* I commit myself to love unreservedly for the sake of God's reign."[15] A powerful mandate, this! Nor does it imply that other Christians do not have similar obligations. Their bonding, however, works itself out according to their call. For married persons, for example, this implies the particularized familial setting that is theirs. Ours works itself out with other women or men, not so much in a coupled as in a communal setting. Community, for us, is primary to celibate loving. The question that keeps haunting me, however, with increasing persistency is why it is that today we find community life in such turmoil. The words of Rahner quoted in chapter 2 come to mind again and seem, I think, particularly pertinent for many of us in the present experience of community: "Face loneliness."[16] Few religious in contemporary communities would argue that indeed loneliness is theirs and, sad but true, even fewer would envision the chance of a healthy transformation of this loneliness into an authentic experience of aloneness or solitude.

---

*I wish to draw attention to this as a countercultural view. Loving today is expected to be smooth, cool, and painless. We fall into it as easily as we fall out of it and, if people do not satisfy our cravings, we can always, as John Francis Kavanaugh points out, "have a Romance with Olivetti," our personal computer, or telephone answering system; or engage in a "Problem-free Relationship" with the latest model car.[14]

What is it that has made community living so frequently a gathering of strangers who meet occasionally for meals, take turns cooking, attend required meetings where they share what they must—often to fill in a report required by the mother house or office of "ongoing formation"—but otherwise pass each other like ships in the night, busy about their ministries but getting slowly and steadily ever more dehydrated except for the occasional reinforcement that comes from ministry support groups? Why has community life for many of us become something that must be "suffered" rather than something that empowers and affirms the vision of our constitutions? It is clear to me these days more than ever before, when ministry is readily available to anyone who desires to serve and no one needs to rely on us for training as such, that new membership in religious congregations will depend largely on how we address ourselves to these questions. Women and men who come to join us are looking for the empowerment in their ministry that our lifestyle in community can make possible. If our life together lacks heart, why would they possibly want to come? For the most part they can do whatever we do in ministry quite well alone. I am convinced that they are searching for that "something more."

And yet Rahner warns us not to give quick answers to depth concerns (and our concerns here are definitely that). In order to probe questions like these reverently, we need to dwell in them rather than assuage their pain with a "quick fix." We need to let the question *be* question, even if that hurts. We need to wait. This can mean feeling very alone at times, perhaps even feeling despair. Too often, claims Rahner, especially in Catholic circles, we want neat definitions, tidy solutions. We have not developed the art of midwifery,[17] and so, very frequently, the answers get aborted. He warns us that, to move into depth experience, we need to *face* loneliness, to *face* fear. We need to endure *ourselves*. We need to let ultimate, basic human experiences surface. We cannot simply talk about them, but must endure them toward transformation.

Unfortunately one cannot be educated "into" or "out of" issues of relationship. Workshops in assertiveness training and direct communication may help, but individuation—that is,

touching the depths of the self and there reaching out in love—
goes deeper than that. Ultimate human experiences of fear and
loneliness, of pain and of growing needs, cannot be programed
out of existence, nor (even with the best intentions) resolved at
community goal setting. Most definitely they cannot be ignored
or denied, for pain does not go away if I refuse to look at it.
They need to be *faced* and they need to be *endured*. For this one
needs time and space. It is of little value for any of us to find
escape in our ministries when matters are too painful at home,
for if we are part of community, its problems cannot be resolved
in our absence. Nor does what I have come to call the "pilgrim
people excuse" hold up when the mandate is individuation: Intimacy and growth issues take time to surface and be resolved.
Whether we like it or not, they need a certain group stability
where members commit themselves to the same community for
several years and thus allow for bonding to occur. For a community whose in and out flow is like a revolving door, or for individuals who change communities every few years or whenever
relationships begin to make demands (even though they may
claim the "Gospel" for an excuse), these issues may never surface
and certainly will not be resolved. We take ourselves and our
unaddressed conflicts wherever we go. No one except each one
of us, "in patient endurance" (Rom. 8:25) can work out our redemption (maturation, individuation). We need a committed
community as our sacred forum for this.

It may console us to recognize that in the struggle for authentic interrelationship we are not alone. Though the ideals of mature interdependence have been around for a while in the
textbooks of human behavior, their existential reality in our time
and in our culture is extremely rare. The worldview of our age,
as was discussed in chapter 1, is still quite entrenched in
dualistic-patriarchal (hence masculinized) values. Although this
worldview seems to be reaching a limit-situation[18] with its consequent experience of alienation and confusion, the new is only
slowly emerging. The consternation many of us feel when we
find ourselves at our wits' end in the face of communal turmoil
and apathy is, therefore, not unique to us. We remember Beatrice Bruteau's call for a genuine "revolution of consciousness,"
a "gestalt shift," as she puts it, "in the whole way of seeing our

relations to one another so that our behavior patterns are re-formed from the inside out."[19] This is a mandate for our culture, not one addressed to religious only. We are caught in the same dilemma as others (married and single alike) whose drive toward wholeness urges them beyond the cultural dysfunctionality in which they themselves flounder.

Unfortunately crises in culture, as well as those of personal maturation, with which they are intimately connected, do not resolve themselves immediately upon recognition. They come upon us and are resolved in their own time. It may help to understand them as events of "cosmic consciousness," ontological in nature: we do not have them as much as we are held in them even as we are summoned to deeper consciousness and consequent transcendence.[20] A certain surrender to the fact, a gentle honesty that prevents us from blindly claiming immunity from global disorder, might be one way of embracing Rahner's invitation to "endure" ourselves. It will also preserve us from the illusion that matters are easier, more "together," in other walks of life (a temptation that tends to be particularly strong during the crisis of the middle years where so many of us seem to find ourselves at present).

Called to Vulnerability

Perhaps in this matter of relationship we need also to accept, once again, the primacy of disposition (something that in an action- and success-oriented world may be extremely difficult). I seriously doubt that community is fostered primarily by what we do in it or about it: with how many persons we live, how often we meet, what we meet about, and whether there is or is not an agenda for the meeting. Although these issues are important, our main concern, simplistic as this may sound, is in the last analysis whether we trust each other; whether we can be vulnerable, poor, in each other's presence; whether there is, when we encounter one another, a basic stance of openness to the self-revelation of God in this meeting. This will allow for community to happen and, whether we consciously admit it or not, we know that nothing else will. Claiming celibacy as a commitment to love each other finds its meaning and place here also. We are not dealing with rules and regulations; with measurable data as to how one should or should not behave. We are embracing an attitude, an open readiness for encounter, a willingness to be met.

The paradox presented here cannot be ignored: We claim that attitude, disposition, is primary to action; without it no amount of activity is going to bring about successful bonding. Yet it is in interaction that attitude is deepened, pruned, empowered, chastised. In interaction life moves us into mature celibacy—into the depth of bonding and of relationship. Perhaps the reflection-action-reflection model, which so many of us have used in discernment processes, can serve as a model to explain this. One could say that our initial openness gets deepened further and matures through interaction. We move from openness to action (interaction), to greater openness. This may be illustrated in the following example:

1. *Disposition:* I come to a new community situation with a disposition based on initial faith-filled trust. I have attempted to leave aside those assumptions, presuppositions, prejudices, and negative memories that may be present in me and of which I am aware. I have tried to "bracket them," so to speak, though it is unreal and unhealthy to resolve to forget them. I simply decide not to let them influence me unjustly. I hope for fresh beginnings, for community built on the conviction that growth is and has been in process in all our lives. Even now, of course, my openness is not total. I, like all of humankind, carry the burdens of my own past—my facticity, my prison walls within. They are often unconscious, buried deep in the denial and repression of past pains: a dysfunctional family, childhood humiliations and abuse, shame of one kind or another, trauma, guilt. Those with whom I relate and interact encounter me out of their facticity also—their openness clouded with unconscious projections, unacknowledged expectations.

2. *Interaction:* We stretch each other. We care for, as well as hurt, each other. Our trust might turn to distrust. We feel rejection, pain. We are wounded. Here it is that our vow to love each other enters into the picture: We embrace the flood of life to which we committed ourselves by this form of relationship, with all the anguish, turmoil, and grace. We allow ourselves to

endure it all, be with it; to let it teach us. *And we pray!* We pray that we might see as God sees and love as God loves. We do not run away from the flood of pain, or busy ourselves with ministerial concerns, but immerse ourselves into a deepened attitude of openness, of trust-grown-wiser.

3. *Deepened Disposition:* And compassionately we walk this earth. Having met, and continuing to meet, our own noonday devil, and knowing how weak we are, we support others in their brokenness. We love.

Taking Ownership of Our Feelings

There may be many different emotions as we move into relationship, into celibate loving, into communal bonding. For those among us who are firmly established in pre–Vatican II training and values, there may be fear, real anxiety. We were never allowed to show our feelings toward others, be they positive or negative. Over the years we have built walls, therefore. We may not even know that we have built them. We may be convinced that our rationalizations are expressions of feelings. Behind them we find ourselves often passively aggressive, obsequious, or gossipy for "sister's or brother's own good." We might come to believe that our silence is virtue, while we are like volcanoes that have never erupted. Perhaps our celibate chastity has never been lived. It may have been avoided instead. For us the emptiness of the "virgin waiting to be filled,"[21] the self-sacrifice of total responsibility,[22] was interpreted as abnegation for its own sake. As such it resulted more frequently in a separation from our deepest center—from that part of us that reverberates with passion and with life—than in a life-fulfilling union. Propriety rather than passion was our guiding principle. We did what was expected of us as good religious. Our guiding force was outside of us. When we now hear talk of bonding and intimacy we feel confused and upset. Friendships in our time were frowned upon and regarded with suspicion. Voicing our views was seen as pride and confrontation, the prerogative of the superior. Relational pain is something we may feel or have felt, yes, but we have none of the tools whereby to acknowledge it. Talk of it, therefore, makes us fearful and nervous.

Then there are those among us who are newer in the congregation. We entered, most likely, *for* community. We have come to bond, to relate. We now want what we came for, and we want it our way. We find it difficult to comprehend why those we joined may be more reticent. We find ourselves impatient with them at times, and perhaps judgmental. We want to say and show what we feel, when we feel it. We often feel passionately and we may discover, if we have not done so before, that as women we can feel this for women, as men, for men. We may not know why this is happening all of a sudden and we may feel guilty and ashamed. We may not know what to do with this. We may confide and then feel betrayed by the seeming lack of response, or the fear, or even the failure of confidentiality. These experiences can be bitterly disappointing for us and result in thorough confusion. We may radically question why we are here and may even want to give up.

There are also those among us who are angry (and perhaps these are the majority). We are angry at a community that never understood us or that understood us too late. We are angry at the church that still does not understand nor seem to care. We are angry at our parents who were alcoholic, narcissistic; who perhaps were poor or died too young; with whom we could never relate and who, therefore, never taught us the skills we now so desperately need. We are angry at the choice we made in life for reasons we may now question. We are lonely and we may wonder what we are now doing here, yet see no sufficient reason for leaving. We may desperately want intimacy but may feel that our life-pattern or the reputation we have been "saddled with" in the institute prevents it. Perhaps behind our anger there also is fear of being hurt in the process.

We bring all these feelings—our fears, our expectations, disappointment, and confusion, our anger and our loneliness—with us into community, into relationship. We rarely leave anything behind and ought not deny any of it. We say one to another in the depths of our hearts as we struggle with our feelings and perhaps with our guilt: "*I am a vowed religious, a celibate woman, a celibate man, moving into evangelical chastity. I am trying to be, in Henri J. M. Nouwen's words, the* Vacare Deo,[23] *the empty space for the breakthrough of God, the virgin mother, as the mystics would see it, the mirror in whom the divine manifests not only himself but perhaps for the first time in my life—because of my struggle for wholeness— herself as well. I can do this only if you help me; if, as we journey together, as we relate and bond, you help me reveal myself to myself and to you as the crucified and the resurrected Christ.*[24] *As I am your com-panion, the one who breaks bread with you, be with me in this, as I will be with you, and I vow not to forsake the quest."*

This is the stuff, as I see it, of celibate loving; of bonding—the bonding of women, of men, in an honest, insightful, and inter-dependent way. It has nothing to do with antiseptic sweetness, with perpetual "niceness," with always being in a good mood and never struggling for availability. Nor does it mean liking everyone equally. It has everything to do with integrity, with commitment, with reverence for diversity and willingness to grow and further growth. It has everything to do with patience and with waiting and with working out the redemption of our emotions and interactions in the blood, sweat, and tears of our existential nows.[25] "The whole world," says Jung, "is God's suffering, and every individual . . . who wants to get anywhere near his [her] own wholeness knows that this is the way of the cross. But the eternal promise for him [her] who bears his [her] own cross is the Paraclete,"[26] the Spirit of life that groans within us.

A woman in labor waits—not passively, but creatively. Our life is a process of birthing, a movement into God, a deliberate, a quiet, sometimes chaotic, often agonized letting be. There are no quick answers or solutions to learning how to live lovingly. There will be the pangs of birth and the joys of birth, and then there will be the dying and the being born over and over and over again.

Celibate loving, holistic bonding, calls us toward honest, dedicated, mutual empowerment in the life-process of maturation and holiness. Anything short of this will, I believe, choke community life and destroy our institutes. Consecrated celibacy, the way it is described here, is the vow of community life. If we dare live it fully, it will, in spite of the contrary claims of our culture, be our vehicle toward wholeness. It will bring us depth and fulfillment, but it will also, and inexorably, lead us through loneliness into the "final solitude" Rahner mentioned, for it will expose us to the radical insufficiency of all human loving and reveal us to ourselves as the living symbols of all of humanity's ultimate and ontological homesickness for God.

Living the Tension

In an article about the famous American poet May Sarton, Kathryn North meditates on Sarton's "willingness to face the challenges of creative solitude."[27] She suggests that Sarton found the rewards of seeking solitude paralleling the rewards found in facing "the challenges of creative relationship," namely, to "move from a state of mere togetherness to a depth experience of *being with* another: what might perhaps be called 'the moment of vulnerability.' "[28] North writes: "It is this vulnerability, this nakedness to the other that allows our human relationships to open out into depth communion, not only with one another at the creative level," and for us this is clearly the ministry level, "but with the Ground of Being at the depth level as well."[29]

Perhaps it is the word "vulnerability" once again, that holds the key for us in this reflection. We have grown so strong. We are so busy now. We have become so good, so professional, at what we do in so many diverse fields. We find ourselves, however, in a functional, efficient world and in a functional, efficient church structure. To be good in it means in many ways to succumb to its values of toughness, of logic, of certainty, exclusivity, ambition, and power. The ways of gentleness, of mystery, of inclusivity, of compassion and vulnerability do not speak in this world, nor in this church. Yet these are the ways of Christ-filled love; the keys to bonding, to mutual empowerment, to companioning, to life-giving community. We stand in the tension, then, of what appears to be the polarity between the professional and a loving community life. A "community for mission," if it is to mean anything at all rather than remain merely a pious platitude, will have to evaluate this tension; examine it holistically in the light of the Gospel, and challenge its possible excesses. Each one of us also, as a member of community and as minister, needs to balance his or her priorities honestly. This challenge is real and it is complex, but it is the challenge of our time. We ignore it only at the risk of our personal and communal integrity.

Some Reflections on Our Existential Situation

We began the reflections of this chapter by suggesting that a community that empowers each one of us to stand in the truth of our own integrity will have to be not only of adults, but also *for* us *as* adults. The "primary family" model will not do any longer, whether our parent figures are superiors, pastors, moderators, coordinators, or just our own sisters and brothers who either appoint themselves or whom we appoint to parent us. Authentic interrelationship demands sensitivity to appropriate emotional distance. Just as religious community is not possible for people who live next to each other without meeting, busy about their separate affairs like atomized apartment dwellers in a metropolitan high rise, it is also impossible for overdemanding grown-up children who have never learned to stand within and accept the poverty of their own authentic personhood,[30] and who, therefore, make the satisfaction of their overblown dependencies the condition for peaceful cohabitation. I suggested Sandra Schneiders' "community of friends who are co-disciples in ministry" as possibly a more appropriate model for adult communities.

The movement, however, into this model cannot be assumed to be easy. It is anything but a simple adult decision. The art of interdependent relating, already mentioned, is "virgin territory" on the map of human development, and though good intentions always help, the day-to-day working out of it is a painful business. The main problem lies, I believe, in the fact that although maturation (individuation) is the business particularly of our adult years, adulthood and maturity do not necessarily coincide. Whereas the former is linear and can be identified with relative chronological accuracy, the latter is a spiraling process that is not so much achieved as it is surrendered to. We are motivated (driven) by the urge to maturation very much as we are motivated (driven) by hunger, thirst, and the desire for happiness. But the stirrings of our urges are not always at our beck and call. With regard to maturation, we can at best be open, willing, and ready. "The wind blows where [and when] it will" (John 3:8) and with the intensity it chooses. Our experience of it, though it always is grace, can sometimes feel like affliction. And so when we enter into a community even with the best resolutions, the movements of our various journeys may bring with them much pain and conflict; and the call to let be, while "becoming" is happening at all kinds of levels, may often be very difficult to hear.

We all come into community life, as into marriage, carrying images from the past still insufficiently integrated. Learning not to project these onto others is a long process. Authority figures are the easiest target, but so is any other person who is powerful, gifted, a leader, manipulative, or simply very different from us. It is a long struggle to the discovery that most of the passions aroused by these issues have to do with my own inner world and conflicts, rather than with the ordinary—or even less ordinary—flesh-and-blood people around me. Few people and institutions have the authority and power our complexes tend to project onto them.[31]

Learning that this is so (withdrawing projections) is, however, an arduous task and we tend to suffer much, often at our own (unconscious) hands.

Encountering the Shadow

Harsh as it may sound, I do believe there is truth in the statement that in many situations we are as oppressed as we allow ourselves to be, both institutionally and personally. In the former case we can often give the letter of institutional regulations much more power than it deserves, simply because we are not willing to risk the freedom of responsible interpretation. In the latter case, is it not true that the oppression in many of our communities comes from dysfunctionality not addressed? How often does Sister X.'s pouting, temper tantrum, weeping, complaining, or gossip dictate our individual or community decisions? How frequently do we yield to the one who talks most or loudest or is the pushiest, and then wonder why community discernment is ineffective? Our fears, anxieties, feelings of inferiority, reluctance to confront, hesitation to speak up, to make decisions, and to take responsibility are, however, as much rooted in an insufficiently integrated past as Sister X.'s temper tantrum or Brother Y.'s pushiness. Furthermore, what we see in others is frequently exacerbated by our very own propensity for the same, though it may have been unrecognized or repressed since childhood, and often clouded by the intentional cultivation of its opposite. A facilitator friend of mine once shared with me her utter amazement at the frequency of projection in conflictual situations: "I sit here," she told me, "and marvel how it is that Brother M. is totally unaware that he is doing precisely what he is accusing his companion of." Jung attests to my friend's observation by a variety of succinct aphorisms recorded by Jolande Jacobi and R. F. C. Hull and well worth our notice:

Our unwillingness to see our own faults and the projection of them onto others is the source of most quarrels, and the strongest guarantee that injustice, animosity, and persecution will not easily die out.

A [person's] hatred is always concentrated on the thing that makes him [her] conscious of his [her] bad qualities.

A [person] who is unconscious of himself [herself] acts in a blind, instinctive way and is in addition fooled by all the illusions that arise when [s/he] sees everything that [s/he] is not conscious of in himself [herself] coming to meet him [her] from outside as projections upon his [her] neighbor.[32]

Jung insists, of course, that those upon whom we project our own darkness (or light, for that matter) are not necessarily without blame: "Even the worst projection is at least hung on a hook, perhaps a very small one, but still a hook offered by the other person."[33] Nevertheless, I think it is safe to suggest that our capacity to perceive both vice and virtue in another is directly proportional to our own propensity in their regard. Awareness of this (our "shadow" as Jung calls it) might do much to foster healthy and compassionate communal interaction and constructive rather than destructive confrontation.

The shadow we encounter in communal living, though its presence appears more often as adversarial, is really, if encountered openly and embraced, a tremendous helpmate toward maturation and integration. Many of us who are walking the midlife journey recognize in this archetype the gatekeeper to the second half of life. To face the hidden and feared dimensions of my personality and yet to survive, even more, to come to know

peace in the encounter and to meet, perhaps for the first time in
my life, my sisters and brothers as companions in the brokenness pours radiance into the darkness and makes redemption of
sin. It furthers authentic maturation. To be sure, the potentials
for growth envisioned here in communal interaction do not
present community as a blissful haven of tranquility, but, as
Mary Wolff-Salin rightfully points out: "If there is no conflict,
no honesty, no shadow, nothing real can be built. But if I can be
able to share with those around me my weakness and pain as
well as my strength, my nastiness as well as my love, perhaps it
is worth the struggle of a less perfect-seeming harmony."[34]

This is not always immediately obvious to mid-lifers, of
course, who feel particularly in need of "some peace and quiet"
even as, often unwittingly, they contribute to their own as well
as communal unrest by the inner turmoil they are experiencing.
Hence, during this time, when an understanding community
may be especially helpful, the temptation to move away from it
is often the most intense. There simply is no way around the
fact, however, that we encounter our shadow primarily in our
interactions with others. The recognition and acceptance of our
essential co-being is probably never as necessary, therefore, as
during mid-life, and it seems tragic to me that now when the
majority of us are in fact experiencing this part of the maturation journey, our community life is often of so little help. The
exodus from community into single apartment living by some of
our most vibrant members (although one does not want to ignore the fact that ministry and personal developmental needs can
very often be a legitimate reason for this) does seem to indicate
that somehow our living together needs to be seriously reexam-
ined if we are sincere about our own personal as well as communal transformation and growth into wholeness. Salin says it
well:

The struggle to withdraw projections and integrate the dark aspects of
reality, to find and get in touch with my own authority while recognizing that of others, the work of coming to terms with the contrasex-
ual—within and around me—all these are necessary steps on the path
toward increasing selfhood and openness to the Self deeper and greater
than my own. *Life together in community can help this process. But it is not
an easy way.*[35]

Reflections on Intimacy

Movement into a "community of friends" also carries with it numerous concrete questions about intimacy. To begin with, we all know that the friendship and bonding to be experienced in our communal living of the vows cannot be expected to be of equal depth with every person with whom we live, nor is it denied, of course, to persons with whom we do not live. Either case would be quite unrealistic; given the human condition, quite impossible, in fact. Personality type, interest, education, and background, life experience, culture, ethnocentricity, and numerous other factors often quite intangible all play a role in drawing persons to each other or keeping them apart. It may be true that we are all members of the same congregation, joined by the same charism and dedicated to furthering the reign of God, but, beautiful as this may be, it is no guarantee that we all will, therefore, like each other or will like each other equally well. The vow of celibacy, as I have tried to reflect on it in these pages, lays stress on our willingness to love one another, not necessarily to be attracted to one another. We are called to immerse ourselves into life with one another: to live it to the fullest, in open responsiveness to relationship with all its beauty and its pain. This immersion will have its dyings and its risings, its closeness and its distance, its positive as well as its negative aspects. Living these means facing them honestly. Openness to relationship does not mean that we can be all things to all people; that we can at all times be present to all members of our community in exactly the way they need or want it. Nor can we expect them to be so for us.

It may be true that in the model of community living in which many of us were trained we used to do everything together, and some of us may in those days even have believed that this implied at-oneness and love. We know today, however, if we did not know then, that there is more to authentic interrelation than getting up together, saying our prayers together, going to school together, eating our meals together, darning stockings together, playing Ping-Pong together, and so on. The physical proximity of my brothers and sisters does not guarantee their presence. Authentic interrelationship points to the latter. This is not necessarily obtained according to the mandates of physical proximity, however, and may even be curtailed, especially if there is too much of it.

All this seems obvious enough and one might legitimately wonder whether it needs to be brought up at all. We have lived, after all, for twenty-five or more years now in community settings quite different from those of the early "formation" of many of us. Today, it would seem, we are hard pressed to find even prayer time together. Yet, it seems to me, that in the area of emotional needs the tendency to claim togetherness as a right in order to avoid real or perceived exclusion, or to see togetherness as a substitute for intimacy and thus to avoid the hard work this entails, is, nevertheless, still prevalent today. What, for example, is it that has us bristle when friends living together in our local communities go out for the occasional dinner or breakfast; when we see them walking together or going on vacation together without us? We, on the other hand, can call our closest friend as frequently as we want and arrange all sorts of outings. As long as one is seen leaving the house "alone," no one in the local community can feel excluded. As childish as this may sound, it is a fact even today that friends will frequently forego living together in order to avoid community pressure and the pain of having to defend their relational needs. Yet the reality is that living life to the fullest means embracing intimacy issues honestly and freely. My community is not my home if I cannot work out at least some of my affective needs there. Nor is the solution necessarily found in coupling off together, away from community. Coupled existence is for another vocation.* Our journey into wholeness includes the working through of our relational issues and should make this possible for us in a communal setting. Yet it is a fact that this rarely happens. Somehow

*I do not mean to imply that the cohabitation of two religious necessarily points to coupling. There can be many reasons why a community may be composed of only two. If withdrawal from larger communal involvement, however, is the primary and enduring reason, and if the desire to be exclusively with my friend predominates, consecrated celibacy is not served. The issue revolves at all times around the appropriate emotional proximity and distance to which our celibate commitment calls us. This needs to be worked out, and friends need time and support to do this. I believe that a loving and honest community can be of great help here.

these matters still seem too painful or too complex for us to address.

I am not suggesting by these remarks, of course, that intimate friendship is a given and ought to be expected or demanded when one moves into community. Intimacy in relationship emerges; it is gift. We are vowed to loving openness toward one another. Anything over and above that is grace and we do little to earn it. Kipling's "Thousandth Man" (or woman) is rare, but blessed, I believe, are the communities that empower this emergence, for in authentic friendship much growth is possible both for the community that supports it and the persons involved. A friend of mine, during a time of deep relational struggle, gave me a verse one time that says it well: "Love, like God, frees us to suffer for one another, makes us primal, creating new selves."

Perhaps it is true that only intimacy allows for intimacy. When our communities become our homes and we can be for each other without fear, intimacy may lose its threat and we may begin to see it as the natural phenomenon of maturation that it is. When we feel fear in the presence of others we usually will want to avoid them; our conversation with them, even if we call it "sharing," is, as Henri Nouwen sees it, flat and noncommittal. Sometimes we create a false closeness: We "talk too long with them, laugh too loudly at their jokes, or agree too soon with their opinions."[36] At any rate, our togetherness is artificial, forced. "Fear prevents us from forming an intimate community in which we can grow together, everyone in his or her own way"; where we can "confess to each other our sins, our brokenness, and our wounds"; where we can "forgive each other and come to reconciliation."[37] Intimacy, on the other hand, allows for space to grow, for littleness and vulnerability and honesty. Authentic friendship is its natural consequence.

Too often, in the past, our overeager attempts to create communities where bonding will happen have led to forced and, therefore, unreal, fear-filled intimacy (a contradiction in terms), or else to complete relational shutdown. Bonding does not happen on command and cannot be planned (not even in "formation" houses). Legislated participation in community affairs and meetings where we expect sharing and demand it of each other (sometimes even with unspoken criteria of measurability: "She

never speaks up. She is probably too lethargic to care") destroys
the emergence necessary for depth relationship. It causes fear.
This does not mean, of course, that if we love each other we
cannot call each other forth and make attempts to involve one
another, but the love *always precedes* the calling forth, not vice
versa, and it is a love that has to be felt, experienced, not just
pronounced:

Sister N., a member of a community of six, is never at home. She
spends her time with her family and her ministry. The sisters see her
getting coffee in the early hours of the morning, skimming the paper,
and then driving off for the day to return too late in the evening for
any meaningful contact. The scheduling of meetings with her is barely
possible. They write her notes to reach her before she leaves again. She
simply is never there. They are distressed and wonder what they can
do to deal with this issue. They get together—the five of them—to
commiserate and decide that something needs to be done. Several of
them have already tried "throwing hints" when they see her: "Oh,
you're home! Well, that's a change!" to no avail. Others have talked to
other sisters they know she knows hoping that they might mention it
to her. Several have individually tried to impress the seriousness of this
matter upon the community life co-ordinator. They come to the conclusion that at the next visitation they will all mention it to the provincial in the hope that she will deal with the matter.

We are all familiar with scenarios like this or similar ones. Our
communities abound with them. What really is the matter here?
If Sister N. is absent and we really miss her, what can the provincial do about it? Could N. not have hundreds of legitimate
reasons for her absence, and would not the provincial's remarks
only intensify her desire to stay away? Who is missing when she
is not at community meetings? Is it her physical presence—that
additional inhabitant of the house that makes for six? I wonder if
any of us have ever thought of talking with (reaching out to) our
Sister N. in similar situations, and of telling her that *we miss her.*
Perhaps we might stay up late one night and catch her during
the eleven o'clock news and share with her somehow that her
presence is important to us: "Sister, I really *miss* you. *I* miss
you." We might tell her that we know she is busy, but would
really so much want to go out to lunch sometime or take in a
movie with her.

I remember using this example when speaking of community and celibacy to a group of sisters not long ago. During the question period a sister wanted to know what one should do if one really did not miss Sister N. That is, of course, quite possible. The reason for N.'s absence may lie, consciously or not, precisely there; but then, on the other hand, her absence, after a while, can also further our indifference. By our vow of celibacy we commit ourselves to love one another. The minimum requirement of this, as I see it, is making ourselves available to be met. The tragedy of our lives together today truly is that so many of us really do not miss each other. I believe one reason for this is that we have never really met.

Our Homesickness for God

In his book *Inner Loneliness,* Sebastian Moore makes the bold suggestion that the desire that can make people desperate enough to move into addictive behavior of whatever kind is really deep down the desire to have their nagging emptiness filled by unreserved, unconditional, unending love; in other words, by God.[38] "In the depths of my ultimate loneliness," he says, "where none can reach me, I want there to be Another whose very 'to be' is 'to be for me', whose selfhood is not a selfhood into which [s/he] must ultimately retreat leaving me to mine." I want someone "constitutionally involved with me, and constitutionally other than me. And this *is* 'what all call God.' "[39] Moore contends that human loneliness for the ultimate, because its intensity can often be quite unbearable, frequently gets displaced. "People try to fulfill *with each other* the insatiable requirement of the inner loneliness, to be totally entered and led forth into the whole ecstasy of existence. That there *is* this need for God in us is shown by the fact that we demand of each other to *be* God for us."[40] The history of human loving is one of unquenchable thirst.

Men and women religious here, as in all other aspects of the human condition, are very much part of history. We might have hoped that joining a community of adults for adults as adults would allow us to escape the pain of misplaced expectations of intimacy and even addictive emotional dependency. This, how-

ever, simply is not the case. It was already mentioned that adulthood does not automatically imply maturity. Maturity, as the
spiraling process I suggested it is, has a tendency, regardless of
the pain, to bring us over and over again into our own past in
order to move us toward ever deeper levels of integration. This
is a difficult concept to appreciate in a culture where "having it
all together" once and for all is the sign of integrative excellence. In my own work I often tell people: "Having it all together means knowing that you don't." This is the truth of
maturation as journey. It is generally messy and excruciatingly
on its own time.

It may help to know that with regard to "inner loneliness"
and the possibility of displaced affect, contemporary religious as
a group are in a particularly vulnerable situation. To begin with,
as Charles L. Whitfield, M.D., estimates, "from 60 to 80 per-
cent of today's men and women religious come from dysfunctional family settings."[41] Many of us, therefore, belong quite
readily among Alice Miller's "Prisoners of Childhood": Women
and men, who because of their parents' inability to parent and to
be for them what they desperately and rightfully needed,
learned early in life to reverse roles, becoming "well-behaved,
reliable, empathic, understanding, and convenient child[ren],"
who for the most part, however, were never really allowed to be
children at all, and who now spend a good deal of their adult life
seeking their lost love.[42] Alice Miller writes her book primarily
for therapists who by their sensitivity and care for the feelings of
others have, in fact, developed the virtues of their affliction but
not without pain: the pain, namely, of facing, of grieving, of
mourning and ultimately of letting go what never was for them
and never really will be. Many religious are, in this respect, like
therapists. They developed in the earliest years of life concernful
attention to the needs of their elders in order to get what little
love they could. Their legitimate needs, however, were never
met. They became like sponges absorbing the pain of others
while their own longing for love remained like an open wound.
Their ministerial concern for and awareness of the needs of others today frequently speaks of the neglect they suffered in their
childhood. They too now need a forum where they can come to
see the futility of seeking in their adult life what they were de-

prived of as children and what will never be theirs in human terms. They need to mourn it and to let it go.

It would, of course, be ideal if these issues were dealt with prior to entry into religious community. The recommendations for counseling certainly help our newer members in this regard. The truth is, however, that their "novice director" may be dealing with the same pain and all its affective struggles still, and so might the provincial and the father/mother general, and so will the newer members as they journey through life, for it is a life issue that rarely gets cleared up quickly. There really is precious little one can do about the human condition except acknowledge it and support others in it, hoping for the same from them. This is what, I have tried to say, "vowing to love one another in community" is all about. Letting-go, as final as it may sound, is not a once-in-a-lifetime decision. We die daily at ever deeper levels of surrender.

A second factor to be considered as we reflect on the particular vulnerability of religious in community today is the fact that the vast majority of active religious in our congregations are either just entering or already heavily involved in mid-life issues. It is during the second journey of life, in particular, that the need for inner integration takes hold of us and our individual stories need literally to be re-membered into our lives. Intimacy needs, which may not have been consciously felt or acknowledged before, or which we may never even have known we had, frequently surface during this time with frightening acuteness. As the authors of *Chaos or Creation* see it, there are a variety of reasons for this:

The growing sense of mortality that creates the common 'last chance' mentality; the recognition of my destructive capabilities that may drive me to long for that one perfect, integral relationship; the emptiness of my personal relationships, or my prayer life (or both), that leave me lonely or empty, and longing for fulfillment.[43]

And, as was already suggested, there are the deprivations of childhood, which have finally broken through the taboos that caused repression of their memory and now come to haunt me, together with struggles to forgive and deep feelings of isolation and inadequacy. These are only a few. The emotional turmoil and confusion, and the agonizing recognition of needs, can at times be almost unbearable. It is not uncommon, therefore, that often deep emotional attachments are formed to help weather the storm; sometimes also, perhaps, to avoid it or postpone it. Religious may quite literally experience the "falling in love" that they never expected for themselves. This can be a real learning experience for them if the support and environment are right, but it can also come as a great surprise and sometimes even as a severe shock, given the nonexclusiveness of the love they vowed. To add to their confusion, they may also discover that the gender of the beloved seems often of little relevance to the feelings they have. The pain and guilt of this experience, especially if it takes genital expression, can frequently be as acute as the fascination is exhilarating. Although someone more advanced in the integration process may, as Moore points out, quite readily see here an infatuation that ultimately points beyond itself, it usually is of little use to suggest this until the person involved can hear it. It may be true, as scholars tell us, that "the sexual drive and the unitive drive (or the religious impulse) in human beings is the same."[44] The discovery of this, however, in one's incarnate being is a long and arduous process.

Nevertheless, religious, trying to make sense of the relational turmoil so prevalent today in community life and out, might at least draw some consolation from the fact that the maturation process and the life-force within us, in spite of the emotional chaos through which we may pass in our experience of it, has an ontological momentum toward the transcendent. Gerald G. May, echoing Moore somewhat and speaking here very much within the context of the holistic paradigm discussed in chapter 1, suggests that all emotional experience is grounded in the same kind of "root" energy of the spirit and toward the whole. He points out, however, that the expression and use of this energy may be distorted because of *insufficient awareness of this*. Referring to the "transmutation of energy" he says:

The experience of emotions as manifestations of raw energy can shed considerable light on the relationship between sexuality and spirituality. If the energy that fires both sexual and spiritual feelings is indeed a common "root" force, the distortions of sexuality and spirituality . . . can be seen as resulting not only from confusions about the *nature of the longing* but also from primary *misdirections* in the processing of emotional energy. Any given stimulus may become connected with either spiritual or sexual associations and thus acquire a sexual or spiritual label. . . .

To some degree, individual intentionality or choice can affect the processing of an initial burst of emotional energy. The extent of this influence is directly proportional to one's *clarity of awareness* of the process of emotional formation.[45]

May's insight may make it less difficult for us to understand why seemingly self-possessed religious, in moments of more acute vulnerability and loss (such as, but not restricted to, the mid-life crisis) seem to lose equilibrium at times and may need particular sensitivity and care. What they experience acutely is the sexual or erotic aspect of the same basic life energy moving through each one of us and more or less capable of being focused, differentiated and channeled or being misdirected and misused on our part. Our presence to them needs to be one of compassionate sensitivity and mature friendship—not to be confused with the amused or even blasé tolerance of our age, which looks at celibacy as misguided or institutionally induced frustration bound to go sour sooner or later.

It is clear that, in an age of sexual idolatry such as ours, blindness to the appropriate use of life-energy is prevalent. The dualism of our culture makes awareness of the holistic momentum of our "root" energy extremely difficult. The resultant exaggeration and distortion that in past decades may have come to the fore as "angelism" or Victorianism is today expressed in eroticism and the immediate satisfaction of all cravings. "It must be right because it feels so good," is our culture's slogan as it seeks fulfillment through instant gratification. It is here where the counter-cultural stance of the consecrated celibate can be extremely significant. It witnesses to a world where the genital expression of love virtually excludes all other relational expressions and where sexuality is degraded by its absolutization. It claims that there *can* be other modes of loving; that there can be intimacy without the exploitation and manipulation to which "appetite" so frequently reduces relationship; that sexuality belongs to an embodied wholeness wherein its expression is holy but need not necessarily be genitally manifested at all times. It speaks of inwardness and of human yearning beyond the human; of emptiness endured to make room for the sacred.

The fact that religious in the past rarely, if ever, discussed or addressed their own sexual nature with any kind of seriousness or depth can, of course, be a disadvantage to their witnessing potential here. It has crippled many of us in our own differentiation and channeling of primal energy and frequently prevents us even now from being able effectively to celebrate and enjoy the powers of celibate loving. We live, as I mentioned already, in an age of sexual promiscuity and confusion. "Sexual liberation" for many means precisely the opposite: compulsive surrender to every genital urge. The notion of celibate freedom often seems to escape us as we are haunted by intimations of neurotic repression, sexual frustration, and even deviance and abnormality in a culture that has mechanized sexuality and devalues intimacy on virtually every available billboard and television commercial. Teresa Bielecki of the Spiritual Life Institute in Colorado, when asked how members of her community deal with physical desire, has offered some interesting observations concerning the experience of celibate freedom:

First of all, obviously, you recognize what's happening. You see it in terms of your ultimate commitment to celibacy, and you don't hate yourself for it, because sexual desire is normal and human; it is a power and a gift. Then you have to deal with it creatively. *You have to recognize that you are free to choose. This is why celibacy has so much to offer our culture. We are free to choose.* People need to know that, because a lack of genuine freedom is killing our culture, killing sexuality, killing marriage, killing love. People feel that every time they experience desire, they have to act on it. There are *other* ways to act on it besides genitally.[46]

With May, Bielecki believes that "sexual energy is the life energy at the heart of every human person. We can choose to exercise that human potential genitally or not."[47]

Not long ago a young man in his fourth year of theology at the seminary stopped into my office for a little self-reflection. He shared with me that day his thoughts and concerns regarding celibacy. There is no question that the compulsory nature of celibacy for diocesan priests is a real struggle generally and conversation dealing with this struggle is not uncommon. What my young friend told me that day, however, was: "On the day of ordination," he mused, "I do not want to be asked about promising celibacy. I want to be at the point where I can volunteer it: 'Oh, Bishop, and by the way, I choose celibacy as my way of living out ordained ministry.' " Somehow this young person saw a lack of integrity in being forced into celibacy for the sake of a ministry. For life to be significant, *we must freely choose it*. No doubt, he will have to make his life's choice over and over again, as all religious serious about their vow do also. Forced celibacy, at best, is meaningless; at worst, it demeans both the person and the creative energy that flows through him or her. Consecrated celibacy embraced freely points beyond itself and bears witness to human interiority. This, most likely, will never be totally without struggle. As Kavanaugh rightly points out:

The pains of relinquishment can be frequent and intense. The physical incompletions felt in intimacy without genital orientation or expression are filled with difficulties, purifications, and an aching vacuum close to the bottom of ones's physical life. Care and carefulness are difficult to express in an integral way, and the sequential struggles found in a life of celibacy are as trying as the struggles in married love.[48]

There is also always the temptation to fill one's emptiness with surrogate loves. Moore's "addictions" can be plentiful. We can easily spend a lifetime as exemplary "celibates" whose sexual abstinence cannot be faulted but whose displaced affective energy hankers after "things, possessions, games, professionalism, achievement, and the collection of trifles,"[49] not to forget the unavoidable "additional member" of every community: television and its countless flights into unreality. Affection that is displaced rather than transformed has us live shallow and dehydrated lives surrounded by the inconsequential. We lack the passion of the real.

A tragic phantasy assails me on occasions of reflection such as this to remind me of my own weakness in this regard. I see myself on my death bed haunted by the indescribable agony of a single regret that can be phrased quite simply in one sentence: "Too late have I loved Thee." Our freedom as consecrated celibates is a serious business. Our lives are destined to point all human longing to its ultimate fulfillment in the heart of God; to give special visibility to what Nouwen identifies as the "inner sanctum," the "holy, empty space in human life,"[50] where intimacy with God awaits all our loneliness and yearnings. We come to an in-depth realization of this, our vocation, only slowly, sometimes all too slowly, and often very painfully—in the stripping of our own lives and the searing of our own hearts to which loving in community exposes us. Our initial motivations go, therefore, through innumerable levels of fine-tuning, agonizing purifications, betrayals, and rededications.

In these last several pages I have tried to reflect on the particularly acute vulnerability of religious today. It is my sense that perhaps precisely because of it, as wounded witnesses, we are called to stand for the "priority of God in all relationships,"[51] to give testimony to the ultimacy of the Holy, the inadequacy of all human loves, and our fundamental homesickness for God. Our prayer must be that at all times God's strength is made perfect in our weakness (2 Cor. 12:9). Thus, we experience our utter dependency on God and it is here that we ultimately find our freedom. Living into this destiny of ours, like living into the sacrament of matrimony for others, is, as I mentioned already, a lifelong task, not an accomplished fact on the day of profession. But it is *our* task. Our call is to embrace it in gratitude and freedom. We are defined by it.[52]

Questions for Focus, Reflection, Discussion

1. Do you agree that the polarity between community and mission has been out of balance in your congregation; that too great a stress is placed on mission and that there seems to be neglect of legitimate community concerns?

2. Is our charism deeper than common apostolic priorities? If so, how so? What are the gathering priorities in your community?

3. "Celibate chastity is my way of immersing myself into the pain and ecstasy of life." What meaning does this statement have for you?

4. Is your experience of community one of women/men *for* women/ men *as* women/men? What does this mean for you?

5. How can our ways of bonding be liberated from the sometimes coercive or prescriptive models we use to create community?

6. Have you experienced community as one of "revolving doors"? Do you use the "pilgrim people" excuse to prevent yourself from having to endure the pain of intimacy and bonding?

7. How comfortable are you with the idea that living celibate chastity is a lifelong task, not an accomplished fact on the day of profession? (This, of course, would apply to the other vows as well.)

8. What are your primary feelings and emotions as you move into living your celibacy relationally—fear, anger, confidence, joy, hope, anxiety, discouragement, and so forth? Why is this so?

9. "Our capacity to perceive both vice and virtue in another is directly proportional to our own propensity in their regard." How has your experience of your shadow been furthered through community living?

10. What has been your experience of friendship in community? Have you felt empowered in your experience of intimacy and have you empowered others? Do you experience friendships as a positive element in community interrelations? What is your view of realistic inclusion here? Have you excluded or do you feel excluded in friendship situations?

11. Has your appreciation of consecrated celibacy been enhanced through mature and serious discussion about sexuality and the channeling and focusing of life energy? If not, would you see this kind of discussion as useful in helping you effectively to enjoy and celebrate the powers of celibate loving?

5

Creative Fidelity

A dear friend of mine some years ago told me that in his view the most creative word ever uttered in the history of humankind was the *Fiat* of the Mother of God. A powerful insight, this; yet, sad but true, for some of us, especially for women today, to experience the full power of it and appreciate its depth may not be possible. When we hear statements of this kind, in fact, they may at first evoke discomfort and perhaps even irritation in us rather than awe. Though many among us still belong to the heritage of May processions and crownings, of sodalities and October rosaries recited during early school years, our relation to the young girl in blue, whom we almost worshiped then, has undergone some serious questioning. The Mary of those years has become somewhat of a stranger to those of us who have come to experience a certain one-sidedness, unwholesomeness in the "feminine" meekness, mildness, weakness, and gentleness with which Mary was idealized during our youth. With Carolyn McDade we would like the myth to die,[1] so that the fullness of personhood, the strength and wholeness of God's Mother and, by extension, our own potential for wholeness, might finally appear, flourish, and be celebrated. To hear of the *Fiat* as "creative," therefore, may initially evoke memories of dualistic phantasies glorifying the submission and passive resignation we hope to have grown beyond and would rather do without.

Elsewhere I have reflected on Ann Belford Ulanov's observation concerning the virtual silence in theological literature and certainly in liturgical worship when it comes to celebrating "Mary as a figure of fierce aggressive capacities who singly held

108

herself open to God's presence, without support of reason or conventions of her culture,"[2] and whose *Fiat,* one might add, came only after she dared press an angel for explanations (something for which Zechariah was struck dumb). In recent years I have discovered that this same ecclesial silence also applies to much of our tradition's interpretation of obedience. In many respects our estrangement from Mary as "woman on the pedestal" has come hand in hand, I believe, with a certain questioning and experimental reevalution of our church's traditional interpretation of this virtue and of the vow we embraced many years ago. In a church where oaths of loyalty are required of pastors and theologians alike, where obedience to the supreme pontiff needs to be promised constitutionally by religious congregations, and where thinkers who dare to express differing views from the magisterial status quo are silenced often without anything even remotely resembling due process, "fierce aggressivity" and a questioning stance are the last qualities one would ascribe to obedience. The present-day official view of this virtue seems to speak much more readily to the interpretation offered in the 1927 edition of a then highly respected theological lexicon, which states: "Very few people are capable of achieving a wholeness of life; thus no better use of their freedom can be imagined than for them to relate to some existing whole and to associate with those above them who have achieved wholeness."[3] This kind of position leaves most of us today alienated and angry. The lexicon sees obedience as "submission to authority, full compliance without questioning motives, the simple telling and presenting of holy things rather than the endless asking and answering of questions."[4] We, however, of contemporary times, seriously wonder what such an interpretation has to offer educated adults who see thinking and questioning as necessary for the meaningful encounter with all aspects of their lives and would, in fact, consider neglect in this area irresponsible and disrespectful.

Perhaps no other vow stands more stressfully at the crossroads of the "turning point" in our culture's self-understanding than does the vow of obedience. Perhaps also no other evangelical counsel is interpreted still (and especially in our present magisterial setting) with as much dualistic rigidity, resisting the chal-

lenge and opportunity of creative rethinking.[5] Perhaps no other
virtue is exalted with such absolutism, evoking individualistic
reactionism in kind and, therefore, closing off all avenues for dialogue and transformation. There seems to be little doubt that
obedience in our church is crucified in the intersection of both
the archaic vertical and the present-day horizontal modes of relationship. It is the victim par excellence of a hierarchism that
cannot as yet yield to the wisdom and sacredness of the community; of a "head" that cannot permit itself to trust its "body"
and therefore runs the risk of losing itself in heavenly phantasies
of grandeur rather than being rooted in reality, with its feet
firmly planted on the earth.

Facing the Crisis

In order to situate ourselves specifically and directly in this
crisis point of obedience today, it may be of value for us to recall
briefly the two major paradigms of spirituality identified in
chapter 1 as having been present in our tradition from the earliest times. The more pervasive of these, we will remember, orig-
inated out of the metaphysical dualism that we as church
inherited primarily from the prevailing Greco-Roman culture of
our early missionary encounters. Its structure even to this day is
hierarchical, accenting comparatives in its view of reality. The
"better than," "higher than," "holier than," and "more real
than" dominates in this worldview over the "lower," more material aspects of reality. That which is closer to the spirit, hence
closer to perfection and, therefore, more "godly" must be
sought after and deferred to. Dualism thrives on perfection priorities. There is a chasm in this spirituality between God and
creation, God and man, and, most definitely, between God and
woman.

Though the metaphysics of Greek thought as it had permeated
the Roman empire in the time of early church expansion was
largely responsible for the pervasiveness of dualism in our tradition even to this day, Sandra Schneiders assures us:

Even among the Jews whose God was close to them in covenant love,
a chasm existed between the human world and the divine, between the

profane and the sacred prior to the Incarnation. Humans bridged that chasm by various forms of consecration. They took profane realities such as space, time, objects, and persons and separated them from profane use in order that they might become go-betweens or mediators between an inaccessible God and common humanity. This separation made these human realities superior to their profane counterparts. The Sabbath, the Temple, the sacred vessels, the priests, the animals for sacrifice, and the Law became—by consecration—sacred rather than profane and superior to ordinary places, times, things, behaviors, and persons.[6]

No wonder, then, that the vision of Jesus was revolutionary! We discussed in both chapters 1 and 2 its egalitarian rather than hierarchical emphasis. In it lay the charism of the early Jesus movement, the "discipleship of equals" in love covenant with one another, and mutually empowered: "I no longer speak of you as slaves. . . . Instead, I call you friends. . . . Love one another" (John 15:15, 17). Though, except for its earliest moments, never again dominant in the church, the spirituality of this second paradigm, nevertheless, was never quite lost throughout our tradition. In chapter 1 we reflected on the message of mystical thought that, though sporadic and often misunderstood and persecuted by a hierarchical system, preserved the insight of a lover God, of universal holiness and wholeness, of human equality and cosmic celebration. Today, also, persons interested in wholeness and justice—those concerned with the liberation of the oppressed, with the emancipation of the feminine, with ecology—point to this vision and call our culture toward transformation.

As we attempt to situate obedience in the intersection of these two paradigms, it becomes clear that critical reflection here may be profoundly unsettling. We discussed in chapter 1 the trauma of crisis and the unwillingness of civilizations to let go of the perspectives through which they have achieved their glory.[7] Rigidity, mistrust, and persecution usually precede all paradigm shifts. Today's obsession with "loyalty" and the present magisterium's virtual rejection of all invitations to dialogue can easily be understood as a case in point. But, as in all other crisis situations of human and cultural maturation, stagnation, the unwillingness to grow, and the intransigent conservation of the past for the sake of "tradition" will lead only to regression and decay. It is time that we face the "drought" of obedience in our church; that we enter into "our quiet little house" and pray for the rain of creativity and new insight lest we wither in the dry spell and die of dehydration.

Authoritarian Obedience

In her classic work *Beyond Mere Obedience,* the noted German theologian Dorothee Soelle identifies the obedience of a dualistic, hierarchical society as generally authoritarian.[8] Its chain of command is linear and one-directional, moving from the one who speaks, who gives the command and is presumed to have insight, to the one who listens, obeys, and is not only presumed, but in fact exhorted to be, if not ignorant of, then at least blind to the significance of the action commanded. He or she is, therefore, for all intents and purposes, irresponsible with respect to its consequences. The one who gives the order is seen to be the superior; the one who obeys it, his or her subject. Diligence, speed, and accuracy in receiving and carrying out the command are prized in the subject, while the content, circumstances, and possible consequences of the action are left to the consideration and wisdom (by the grace of state) of the superior.

Soelle introduces this model of obedience by citing an autobiographical account written by a German Catholic born in 1900 and raised in a strictly Christian tradition:

I was brought up by my parents to give due respect and honor to all adults, particularly older persons, no matter which social classes they belonged to. Wherever the need arose, I was told, it was my primary duty to be of assistance. In particular I was always directed to carry out the wishes or directives of my parents, the teacher, pastor, in fact of all adults including household servants, without hesitation, and allow nothing to deter me. What such persons said was always right. *These rules of conduct have become part of my very flesh and blood.*[9]

As a child, this writer tells us, he "was brought up to *obey every command without question,* to be neat and orderly in all things, and to keep scrupulously clean."[10] In Soelle's view:

"Obedience to the voice of command," learned early in life, "subordination to authority," practiced until it becomes habitual, "complete submission of one's own will to the will of another which demonstrates itself in action," in short, obedience as the cornerstone of religious education and as the key concept of the entire Christian message, is a commonly accepted Christian principle.[11]

Though the biographical example cited above has its origin in German Catholicism, Soelle suggests that Protestants and Catholics alike fostered this model of obedience. The author of this example was Rudolf Höss, the director of Auschwitz from 1940 to 1943.[12]

Without succumbing to any simplistic cause and effect theory linking German Catholicism to Nazi atrocities, we have to admit that Soelle presents here a serious indictment of a view of obedience that can no longer be tolerated with impunity. Stanley Milgram's behavioral study of obedience conducted in the 1960s at Yale University,[13] as well as brutalities executed on command against innocent citizens in the war-torn countries of so-called civilization everywhere, attest to the fact that concentration camp violence under orders is not unique to the German psyche. Neither nationality nor ethnicity creates blind obedience, only a certain abnegation of responsibility and unwillingness or inability to assume personal autonomy and to balance external orders with one's own conscience. Soelle is right when she observes that it is up to historians and, I would add, social scientists to determine the level of influence Christian training in obedience had in creating these behavioral monstrosities.[14] Nevertheless, the theologian of this century may no longer look at the notion of unquestioning obedience with innocent eyes, let alone hold it up as virtue—not, at any rate, if that theologian lives with any authenticity in history.

I suspect that we Christians today have the duty to criticize the entire concept of obedience, and that this criticism must be radical, simply because we do not know exactly who God is and what God, at any given moment, wills. It is no longer possible to describe our relationship to God with a formal concept that is limited to the mere performance of duties. We cannot remove ourselves from history if we wish to speak seriously about God. And in our Christian history, our history of the 20th century, obedience has played a catastrophic role. Who forgets this background or conveniently pushes it aside and once more naively attempts to begin with obedience, as if it were merely a matter of obeying the right lord, has not learned a thing from the instruction of God called history.[15]

Any kind of interpretation of obedience that refuses to understand culture, history, sociological data, and social responsibility is today simply unconscionable. One may not hold on to, and certainly not recommend, what clearly can lead to dysfunctionality and irresponsibility. Nor does the free choice of blind obedience in the name of humility or for the sake of "God's glory" alleviate the seriousness of betraying one's own mandate to mature behavior.

It is a known fact that blindness to the total picture—to the implications and ramifications of the act involved—ultimately results in blindness to the authority who commands the action as well. If content is ignored, anyone can command me and, whereas this may, at one time, have been considered desirable (in religious communities, parishes, or dioceses where humble acceptance of whatever superior "God had ordained for me" was lauded as virtue and was, in fact, very convenient to the system), in the broader sphere of human behavior and the development of attitudes, this blindness to Christian superiors easily leads to the same with respect to military, political, or economic superiors. What I am suggesting, in other words, is that, since the emphasis is on the structure of the act rather than the content, religious authority is easily replaced with state, party, market force, or any other system that follows along the same principle.[16] The easy acceptance of totalitarian rule by some of the most Catholic countries of our century speaks for itself. And in America the simplistic (albeit often unconscious) identification of culture with God and all that is holy, which blindly rejects any criticism of American values as unpatriotic, is a blatant indication of the malformation of conscience that blind and unthinking acceptance of our "heritage" and its rules of conduct has led to. My fear is that the Oliver Norths are not an exception here as much as they are a symptom of something much more prevailing. North's popularity among the masses would seem to confirm that in his basic stance he is not alone. Jim Wallis puts it well when he observes:

In the U.S. churches, it is not the kingdom of God that is at hand; it is the American culture that is at hand. It is the social, economic, and military system of the United States. . . . Our conformity to the culture has made the fullness of the teachings of Jesus incomprehensible to many.[17]

The Consequences of Authoritarian Obedience

Conditioned blindness, whether for the sake of God or simply out of fear of punishment or the desire for reward, also invariably leads to lack of self-esteem and ultimate self-deprecation. Looking for one's center always outside of oneself inculcates a basic sense of unworthiness, distrust of self, as well as subservience to those "better," "more qualified," "older," "male" or, quite simply, "called" to be above, to be superior, and therefore to counsel and to guide. It may in some cases even be doubtful whether, after lengthy exposure to the conditioning effects of blind subservience, there remains a self to distrust. Authentic growth demands "movement from an orientation toward heteronomy [finding the law outside] *through autonomy* [having an inner law] in order to reach an ultimately mature, free relationship to God"[18] and the human community generally.

I suspect that one of the reasons why the community of adult friends we discussed in the previous chapter is so difficult to come by in religious life today is quite probably the lack of authentic autonomy from which many of us are still suffering. Truly and genuinely to have found our inner law is more than having attained independence from the demands of superiors or even from each other. It means, above all, having encountered our past and faced there the unfulfilled needs as well as the voices of our childhood: those inner authority figures that haunted us deep into adulthood and, for years, simply spoke to us through our superiors or allowed themselves to be displaced onto the people around us. Authentic autonomy comes when we can acknowledge the extent of our capabilities and accept our essential co-being hand in hand with our uniqueness. When, in other words, we experience interdependence.

That conditioned blindness was very much part of our religious "formation" prior to Vatican II will probably not be denied by anyone. To be sure, it affected some of us more so than others and particularly sensitive personalities steeped in it for years may even today be incapable of retrieving the personal center and inner authority so necessary for healthy adult interaction. These persons are "victims" of the system of coercion that, though freely chosen, nevertheless stood against the very meaning of freedom. Today they walk the halls of our community houses looking for someone to give them permission. Any opinion proffered by anyone asked becomes their dictum and often even their order, their "obedience." They agree with anyone and dialogue or argument confuses them. A "good" religious, after all, does not disagree. Strong-willed persons easily control them. They suffer much.

But we do not have to look for such extremes to find the consequences of authoritarian obedience in our lives. They can be much more subtle and infiltrate our modes of thinking and acting when and where we least expect them. We might, for example, quite honestly find ourselves among those strongly attracted to more holistic paradigms of obedience for today; we might even try to live accordingly and to form community by their standards. But what happens to us when the "crunch is on" and difficult decisions need to be made? We might test ourselves then to see how readily we revert back to the old phrases: "But if I were *really* obedient, I would do what I am asked to do. If I were *really* obedient, I would do what is more difficult or what I don't want to do because others, authority, my community ask me to." It is one thing for us to give intellectual assent to more holistic models for obeying; it is quite another to have a "conversion of consciousness" and to live actively that way, seeking out leadership that will empower us to move from the model of primary family, discussed in the previous chapter, to a mature standing within the integrity of our own being; to say to a leader: "we want you to empower us toward the depth of our own responsibility," instead of "we want you to tell us what to do, to decide whether we have a vocation, what ministry we should apply for, or even how we are to interpret the constitutions."

Reactionism is probably the most subtle result of oppression and a sign of unresolved authority issues. When persons have been kept at childhood levels of responsibility far beyond the chronological limits, a dam of unresolved but potent energies breaks forth once oppression is lifted. Blindness to all legitimate authority can easily follow, and communal chaos is its consequence. Most of us have become aware during recent years (when the experimentation phase after Vatican II had lasted long enough for us to identify valid results) that governance in many local communities is in serious crisis. When everyone among us decides everything, nothing may get decided. It seems obvious enough that consensus is not necessary concerning every mundane detail of our existence. Yet, how upset some of us get when even minor decisions are made in our absence. We waste much time and energy by our unwillingness or fear to call forth our sisters and brothers to serve in leadership according to their gifts. The near paranoia with which some of us approach the issue of community decision making leads one to suspect that our visions and expectations of leadership, despite our outward appearance of independence and maturity, are often clearly still authoritarian (heteronomous) in style, and that a true experience of interdependence has not as yet graced us. We may want to recall our discussion in chapter 2 concerning a holistic approach to leadership, seeing it as a needed gift whenever people are gathered together toward a common end.[19]

Co-authority and Co-responsibility

After this rather painful reflection on authoritarian obedience and its consequences, it is refreshing but also sobering to refer to Sandra Schneiders' to-the-point observation:

What the religious does then, in vowing obedience, is to commit himself or herself without reserve to the seeking of the *will of God* in all circumstances and to fulfilling it with wholehearted dedication not only because one's own holiness lies in this total obedience to God but also in order to extend the reign of God in this world.[20]

It is clear that the universal call to wholeness experienced in a "community of friends who are co-disciples in ministry" cannot be linear and one-directional. As a "discipleship of equals" who are in love-covenant with one another, we are all responsible for

actively seeking the will of God and fulfilling it wholeheartedly.
Speed and blindness in carrying out commands need to be replaced, therefore, by the virtues of listening and mutuality, as we
become aware in ever-deepening ways that God reveals God's
self unconditionally to the attentive heart and that all of us are
expected to listen to the message and respond to it. Authority,
which formerly was seen as the guardian of responsibility, is
thus embraced as co-authority, and responsibility for choices and
decisions made is shared.

Soelle sees the holistic model for obedience as trinitarian in
nature, operating within the interconnectedness of, first, the one
who asks obedience (always God); second, the one who is obedient (the individual, community, and designated authority);
third, the content of obedience itself. Living responsibly in the
world implies sensitivity to the situations demanding action on
behalf of God's reign. This sensitivity is at all times in a discerning posture with regard to content. It is important for a serious
appropriation of the holistic paradigm to recognize that authentic obedience on the part of all people involved embraces the
dual responsibility for answering the one who asks for the action
and taking ownership of what one is asked to do. To overlook
this and to regard obedience simply as monolinear—directed
only to the person "representing" God—means reverting back
to dualism and consequent irresponsibility. The will of God is
discovered within the situation. It can be found nowhere else.

Holistic obedience exhibits concrete involvement in the lived
reality of the moment. This implies the totality of circumstances
and can in no way isolate the action and its urgency from the
ones who ultimately perform it, as if the health, disposition,
gifts, and talents, as well as general condition of individuals,
were irrelevant. Hesitations that, in the past, were so frequently
dismissed as "weakness of faith" to be surrendered to the instant
remedy of the ever present "grace of state," are taken seriously
and explored together when co-authority becomes co-
responsibility. God asks neither the ridiculous nor the impossible. Watering sticks in the blind faith that leaves will sprout, like
scrubbing floors with a toothbrush, may appear desirable in a
system that values blind submission (be it religious "formation"
of the past or military training even today), but neither practice

fosters responsible obedience for the sake of justice and wholeness. Nor do any of us today benefit from having such practices
or their like held up to us as laudatory examples of obedience in
the founding days of our congregations. If the spirituality of that
time made such actions possible, the virtue of patient endurance
in the face of unjust oppression, much more likely than authentic
obedience, should be reflected upon.

In our days the remnants of this sort of oppression creep into
our discernment, whether we know it or not, every time we
choose to overwork someone for the sake of just one more need,
or when we ask persons to live under excessive stress for the
sake of "filling" a community house or saving on transportation. It is a blatant perversion of theology to insist that what is
painful, disagreeable, or feared is necessarily holy or conducive
to holiness, especially when it is asked of us by our superiors;
that it should therefore be cheerfully endured and sought after.
Though working for the reign of God may quite readily involve
sacrifice, the sacred is not designed to be excruciating. Furthermore, as Brennan Manning puts it so well: "God's grace always
precedes [God's] call."[21] Authentic Christian obedience is a
trust-filled dwelling in that fact, and a celebration of the goodness of a Lover-God who wills our happiness and the well-being
of all of humankind. There is in the disposition that comes with
holistic spirituality the "calm, arcane assurance that the grace for
the next step in the Spirit is already there, given.[22] Thus, we
gather to explore together the reality of the situation and how,
as well as by whom, God's reign might best be furthered in joy
and peace.

Autonomous Obedience

Already in the Old Testament we find that content—the act
and the situation that elicits it, its circumstances and consequences—is most important. In Micah 6:8 we read: "You have
been told . . . what is good, and what the Lord requires of you:
Only to do right and to love goodness, and to walk humbly
with your God." The primary mandate for our obedience is doing justice and loving goodness. Soelle assures us that "in the
Old Testament obedience is always related to justice. Under no

circumstances is it related to the ruler in a completely authoritarian manner."[23] The ruler's task was to do justice and to empower others to do the same. Prophets warned him if he betrayed his calling. Theirs was the task of calling him back to his own integrity, to the obedience he owed to the voice of conscience within, to autonomous obedience. We are dealing here with something profoundly creative that has nothing to do with blind submission to orders and everything to do with personal responsibility. "The obedience requested of people is directly concerned with shaping the world entrusted to humans," making it into "a human society in which justice is realized.[24] Biblical obedience is transformative not preservative. Its energy lies in process. It is future directed. "Where the world is understood biblically, that is, as moving toward an end, a goal, an authoritarian obedience cannot adequately express the will of God for the world. It is interested solely in the preservation of order and consequently displays hostility toward the future."[25] It threatens and destroys all that arises out of the creative center of authentic human autonomy.

Authoritarianism and the obedience it demands arises from what I have come to call "serpent consciousness": the direct result ("punishment") of original sin.[26] It thrives on subjugation and control for the sake of nothing but the stagnation of the status quo, often misleadingly referred to as "law and order." A consequence originally of a state of "uncenteredness" (of disobedience, i.e., being scattered in one's listening, hence being unable or unwilling to hear the law within and acting on it; being, therefore, out of focus, harmful to oneself and others), this "serpent consciousness" is obsessed with externally enforced rules requiring heteronomous obedience. The curse of the serpent was to be crushed. Unredeemed dissipation, which knows no other law but outside control, experiences this crushing. It may even hold it up as necessary, since it has never encountered its deeper self, inner directedness, and strength—the freedom, as it were, of the children of God. Both ego-enhancement (the will to power) and the self-deprecation flowing from this dissipation further the "crushing" of the curse. The latter needs it to get direction; the former, to build itself up as ruler, superior, chief.

The freedom of redemption, on the other hand, calls us home to the law written in our own hearts and found in centered listening—in the autonomous obedience modeled for us by Jesus and called for, already before him, by the prophets throughout Old Testament history.

In modern times perhaps no greater testament to the glory as well as the paradox of Christian freedom, to the inner autonomy to which all of us are called, can be found than Dostoyevsky's parable of "The Grand Inquisitor."[27] This man would have enslaved all in order to give to all the benefits of the prison of security. When he encounters Jesus revisiting his church centuries after its founding and in the midst of its inquisitorial excesses, he brands him a heretic bound on disturbing the status quo for which his church had labored assiduously during the centuries after his death. The crime for which the Inquisitor condemns the founder of Christianity consists of reintroducing freedom; of forgetting that humans prefer "peace, and even death, to freedom of choice in the knowledge of good and evil." The Inquisitor admits that "nothing is more seductive for [someone] than his [her] freedom of conscience, but nothing is a greater cause of suffering.[28] In his accusations against Jesus he raves on:

And behold, instead of giving a firm foundation for setting the conscience of [humans] at rest forever, Thou didst choose all that is exceptional, vague and enigmatic. . . . Instead of taking possession of [human] freedom, Thou didst increase it, and burdened the spiritual kingdom of [humankind]with its sufferings forever. Thou didst desire [a person's] free love, that [s/he] should follow Thee freely, enticed and taken captive by Thee. In place of the rigid ancient law, [humans] must hereafter with free heart decide for [themselves] what is good and what is evil, having only Thy image before [them] as [their] guide.[29]

The redemptive "crime" of Christ Jesus, according to Dostoyevsky's Grand Inquisitor, was to model for us the freedom of autonomous obedience, to ask us to listen to the law of the heart and thus to open us up to the turmoil of our own conscience. For this he was bound and imprisoned; for this his tormentor planned to burn him at the stake the following day. Yet, paradoxically, precisely for this also, and because of Christ's mandate that all of us embrace our freedom, even if by it we betray him, Jesus lovingly and without condemnation moved toward his oppressor while they were facing each other in the prison cell and, after he had gently kissed him on the lips, walked back out into freedom, leaving him to his own responsibility.

Even if we would reject him, Christ would have us free. As the free victim of our freedom, he stands at the center of authentic human existence. He is the living truth about freedom as the necessary condition for God's creative love realized in human history. The Christian philosopher Berdyaev explains the paradox presented as follows:

Free goodness involves the freedom of evil; but freedom of evil leads to the destruction of freedom itself and its degeneration into an evil necessity. On the other hand, the denial of the freedom of evil in favour of an exclusive freedom of good ends equally in a negation of freedom and its degeneration—into a good necessity. But a good necessity is not good, because goodness resides in freedom from necessity.[30]

Any interpretation of obedience that turns Christianity into coercion betrays the truth that is Christ. And yet, "enforced goodness" has been part of Christendom almost from its inception. The "crushing" of the curse is very much part of our history even to this day, and here we too can respond only with a "kiss," for counter-oppression is oppression also and does not serve our freedom as children of God.

For anyone who gives these considerations the serious attention they need, it soon becomes clear that the inner freedom with which Jesus embraced the truth of his own integrity is easier to reflect on than embrace, yet in this lies above all else our way home to God. The nature of God's creative love demands of us that our response be free, for love dies when freedom ceases. This is what the kiss of Dostoyevsky's Jesus symbolized. Far from indicating weak niceness in the face of unkindness or cruelty, it came from a disposition of inner strength and quiet self-directedness. It was the kiss of freedom that allowed others their responsibility. Given by the God-man, it would bless even the Inquisitor's unfaithfulness, rather than coerce his loyalty. It would not protect him, however, from its ultimate consequences. The "kiss" was given for the sake of a greater good, namely, love that, without freedom, could not be.

Creative Fidelity

To live into the truth of this can be agony. Only a deep centeredness can endure the pain. It seems to me that often, perhaps because of this pain, many of us spend our time at the periphery of obedience, worrying about its structures and allowing ourselves to be oppressed there, rather than moving into its depth. I do not wish to deny the importance of our concerns with matters of governance and the proper chain of command, and the like. I wonder, however, why they seemed to play such a minimal part in the obedience of Jesus. As Soelle remarks: "Neither the traditional reflection on the how of obedience nor the direct relationship between the one who demands obedience and the one who obeys plays an immediate role" in his life and in his teaching.[31] Whether persons making the request were duly appointed authorities or not was never as important as the inner authority with which they spoke and out of which they lived. Jesus, himself, is our primary example here. Was he not simply the carpenter from Nazareth? Yet power went out from him. People "were spellbound by his teachings, for his words had authority" (Luke 4:32). I cannot help wondering whether, especially for those of us vowed to evangelical obedience in religious congregations, the inwardness of Jesus' obedience will not have to receive a much stronger focus than it seems to have up to now, if we are to survive the "crushing" experience of ecclesial traditionalism. A quiet centeredness that draws from inner strength can, I believe, weather arbitrary high-handedness much more effectively than angry demonstrations for the sake of "making a point." Autonomous obedience may even at times require heteronomous disobedience for the sake of God's reign, which always includes the well-being of humankind. In all this, however, centered listening, communal discernment, and a sincere desire to follow the movement of the Spirit in our lives and in history are the test of authentic freedom. Institutionalism and the worship of law and security are not. "The [law] was made for humans, not humans for the [law]" (Mark 2:27).

It seems to me that, once the cultic interpretations of patri-
archism have been removed from the redemptive designs of
Jesus,[32] there is precious little left of the preordained and fixed.
The obedience of Jesus was much rather a listening-in-process
than an accurate following of orders or of a preexisting ground
plan. As such it was futuristic, creative and so must ours be.
"Where the divine will is thought of as fixed, that which is considered divine is of necessity misunderstood as anchored in the
past—an establishment, a homeland, a right of possession,"[33]
tradition and holy customs. Life lived holistically does not ignore the past, of course, but it will not allow itself to be lost
there, not even by the demands of a "holy rule," or of a magisterium. Only when we respond creatively to the will of God, as
it is revealed to us in the existential situation of the concrete moment, does obedience become alive in us. Then we can listen
with excitement to the possibilities for the transformation of the
world that reveal themselves to us for our response.

If a person is restored to freedom through the liberation of Christ,
[s/he] will not merely accept responsibility for the order of the world;
[s/he] will engage in transforming the world. The power [s/he] needs
to change things, to discover, to invent, to set things in motion, is
spontaneity. This spontaneity in turn inspires new freedom. Persons
who grow up in this life cycle are *not trained to find their place in a given
order,* but to practice freedom.[34]

The spontaneity of creative freedom ought, in no way, be misunderstood as a free-for-all. Creative fidelity to the will of God
revealing itself in the lived reality of the here and now requires,
rather, acute sensitivity: the readiness of the "prudent virgin,"
the fastened belts of servants waiting to serve. Freedom without
obedience is not freedom. It becomes license instead. The depth
disposition of listening openness requires discipline and a willingness not only to give of the self at any moment for the needs
of the situation, but also to wait and to serve the silence; to endure the darkness of that moment until insight on how to act
graces us. The power of authentic obedience lies first and foremost in the depth and surrender of the human heart sensitized
by patient endurance. Once again, this is not something we resolve to "do" in one flash of inspiration. It is rather a call whose
growing edge usually remains a good distance ahead of us.

Unifying Force for All Three Vows

The reflections of these past several pages may appear foreign in many respects to an age that values accuracy and expeditiousness. What does "listening-in-process," after all, have to do with practical efficiency? There seems, however, no way around the fact that what energizes our spontaneity for the obedient freedom exemplified in the Gospels is nurtured not so much by feverish planning and doing, as by humble waiting. The "active" life of Jesus followed only after thirty years of such waiting. Is it not possible and even probable, given especially the drought of our time and our radical need, in so many respects, to gather ourselves in and "pray for rain," that the answers of contemporary revelation lie much more likely in deeper questions—in the mandate to stand radically in the service of truth as mystery and to endure the pain?

What if for each one of us today obedience meant first and foremost attentive openness to the signs of our time and faithfulness to our own integrity as it unfolds? What if the practice of obedience were today more frequently found in the courageous encounter with doubt and with the possibility of faith experienced therein, than with staunch declarations of certitude followed by clear-cut actions? What if obedience meant for us the patient standing in the tensions of seeming moral opposites and enduring the agony of ambiguity? What if we found ourselves, for the sake of the Gospel, having to choose against all our heart's desire and having to bear the pain in silence because no one would understand? What if obedience pointed to bitter endurance of the void; listening into the silent darkness of contemporary faithlessness and letting oneself go in hope, unconditionally, into questions that seem to have no reply? I have already suggested that in an age of technology, of quick as well as accurate replies, it is immensely difficult to assume an attitude of waiting; of standing in the pain of the questions and not demanding a resolution, of reverencing the unfathomable. It is difficult even more so; it is agony, in fact, "to face the issues of our time and to wait in humility for the proper questions wherewith to address them."[35] Yet it is here, precisely in this difficulty, where the paschal mystery opens up for us; where the

sacrifice that is Gospel living, far from the hair shirt and chain
mentality of previous times, blossoms forth from the inside and
heralds redemption. It is here also, I believe, where depth obedience becomes the unifying force for all three vows, and where
authentic Christian community lights up for us as a possibility.

How can we possibly know *poverty* as "solidarity with the poor," for
example, unless we can *wait* in reverence and in pain for the revelation
of that poverty which permeates our very beings: a poverty which
opens us up to humble listening and serving and prevents us from en-
gaging in works of pity instead of mercy. How can we live relationally
as celibates . . . and, therefore, counterculturally, unless we can allow
ourselves to face the uncomfortable questions concerning our own inner darkness; unless we can face the mysteries of the contra-sexual tendencies present in each one of us . . . and admit to our ever ready
willingness to project these upon those whom we encounter? Finding
the truth concerning our inner selves as cobeings means living the
questions toward the deeper insight of further questions encountered in
our reflective being together with others.[36]

It means living in community. It means being obedient. Authentic obedience requires poverty of spirit. It means self-
sacrifice: that "act of total responsibility" we discussed in
chapter 3, "whereby we take complete hold of ourselves and
place ourselves at the disposition of the whole" in order to " 're-
present' the whole."[37] Through self-sacrifice autonomy is safe-
guarded in its integrity. It does not deteriorate into ego-centric
individualism but sees at the center of human interiority a
deeper law that points to our oneness with all of humankind,
with our earth, with the cosmos and ultimately and intimately
with God.

Authentic obedience also requires the emptiness of "virgin
motherhood," the *Vacare Deo* reflected on in chapter 4, the vulnerability that can acknowledge need and let God be God in
us.[38] If we lack emptiness and are full of answers to every situation and for every problem, we cannot possibly be released
enough to listen, neither to one another, nor to God. There is
too much noise inside of us to hear the gentle breeze of the
Spirit. We have the answers before the questions are asked and
find ourselves unable to endure the creative tensions of possibil-

ities. For us obedience would be too risky, too painful and, conscious of it or not, we, therefore, prefer to oppress or be oppressed.

Fiat People

It is interesting that Jesus, the obedient one, the free listener who spoke and acted with inner authority, was most at home with the *anawim*, "the truly and utterly poor before God,"[39] who were poor and knew that they were poor; who, therefore, could also be obedient—empty receivers of the Word, of the energy of God. Their emptiness allowed for "virgin motherhood," for bearing God to the world, because it pointed them to the source of their power and, in their poverty, they abandoned themselves to God. Their justification did not come from doing the proper thing promptly, but from being vulnerable before God and from solely depending on God's power to work itself out in their surrender. They were *fiat* people, involved in what Sandra Schneiders calls "a kind of existential humility,"[40] which counted on nothing other than the infinite mercy of God, and in turn walked this earth with compassion, never judging or condemning, let alone deciding for anyone. Because of their profound sense of littleness and brokenness, as well as their experience of the unconditional acceptance and love of God, the *anawim* through the ages have known that, though the law can be useful, obedience to the law does not make for holiness. Holiness comes with openness to the "Spirit of wisdom, prayer, love, pressing zeal, the very Spirit of Jesus. . . . It is not the law which will tell us what is good (or that we are good); it is our constant seeking of the good which will enable us finally to discern what, in our human affairs, is truly God's will."[41]

Authentic, Christ-liberated obedience flows out of the willingness to let go—a willingness with which we are gifted when we encounter ourselves as *anawim*, as God's poor. As long as we have our talents, strengths, intelligence, position, and power to hold on to, we will continue to compare ourselves and set standards for ourselves and others. Only by embracing and allowing ourselves to be embraced by the radical emptiness of Jesus can we let God be God for us and in us. In this lies our redemption, our homeward path. It is the path that leads to the recognition of our utter incapacity to do anything good by ourselves, and to our acceptance, at last, of God's unlimited love. It is the path that expresses the truth of the human condition as *loved* and as *free*.

Lately I have wondered whether the twentieth century, which has revealed itself to us as so utterly without answers, as the age of alienation, where none of the "old" ways seem to work anymore, as the age of despair and nihilism, may not also ultimately be the age that most readily invites us to radical Gospel obedience. Perhaps for the first time now, when ready-made solutions simply no longer work, when answers prove as many times ineffective as they prove effective, when radical doubt has replaced radical certainty; perhaps now we will be driven by our sheer inability to do much else *to abide in the question and to wait;* to have the question lead us to the depth of inwardness so that we might dwell there in humility and in hope for the birthing of God in our lives.

In the light of these considerations it may now be possible to reflect once again on the *fiat* of God's Mother mentioned at the beginning of this chapter. It may have become clearer now that, far from being a word of passive resignation and meek submission, Mary's yes unleashed extraordinary power. It allowed God's energy to become flesh. Her *fiat* was the testament of her obedience, of the creativity that flows from self-emptying. It gave witness to her courageous surrender to unspeakable difficulties, innumerable questions, and to her utter trust in God who would see her through. Mary is a model of the incredible daring that obedience demands. Through her yes the Christification of the cosmos was made possible; the Word was made flesh and history became significant. Her obedience was powerfully creative, a hallmark of freedom. Yet she had no need to speak of it or even to justify herself in the face of possible rejection. She quietly held these things in her heart in utter releasement. The *fiat* of the Mother of God is for the strong. This means, paradoxically, for those vulnerable enough to give their lives for the transformation of all things in Christ.

Some Reflections on Our Existential Situation

The paradoxes that reveal themselves to us when we probe the depth of obedience are staggering: vulnerability is strength; surrender opens us to freedom; creativity lies in fidelity; obedience must sometimes be disobedience. Powerful insights, these, but for many of us frustratingly "useless." It seems that speculations into their practical significance for our lives as religious in the twentieth century will yield few tangible results. Paradox, it is true, is peculiarly impractical, as well as hopelessly nontheoretical; and when it graces us, it usually reveals nothing until it has moved us to a different kind of "order." One way to learn from it here, may be to direct ourselves very intentionally once again to the "drought" of our times and to remember what the rainmaker of Kiaochau modeled for us. As the story goes, the Catholics, the Protestants, as well as the Chinese, all had their solutions for the drought, but none of them brought rain. Then a dried up old man gathered himself into a quiet little house and "waited." Obedience, more than any other virtue, is first and foremost disposition. In Kiaochau the Catholics, the Protestants, and the Chinese spend a lot of energy "doing." The Catholics *"made* processions,“ the Protestants *"made* prayers," the Chinese "burned joss-sticks and shot off guns." The dried up old man, however, *waited* and through his waiting brought them rain. To wait means to listen, to be open, to be vulnerable, to be poor, to know dependency and, therefore, to point beyond. Often when we wait we are visited by pain, by longing. Waiting implies humble expectancy, creative receptivity, obedience. To wait means to pray.

Prayer

We will remember Jean Shinoda Bolen's observation that the "drought mentality" of the psyche signifies dis-ease, anxiety caused by a lack of inner order; a feeling of isolation, of separation from the whole. In an extraverted world where action needs to bring results, and anxiety and worry run high, where few have time enough to move inward, let alone stay there, viewing our vow of obedience as commitment to prayer-filled centering for the healing of the human family can be very significant.

So often, it seems to me, we also *do* too much when we pray. We "say" our prayers. Even when we come together, we "make" prayer—someone always gets to *do* the prayer service. Personally I often feel quite guilty when I become aware of how bored I get during the fifteen or twenty minutes before every gathering when we *do* our praying.

When prayer services replace the Eucharist, we work especially hard to make them symbolically significant. There is something about ritual, however, that seems to move between the old and the new, and shuns too much variation all at once. Ritual that is too original and, therefore, foreign to many of the participants, tends to distract and move us outward, away from ourselves and even, sometimes, from each other. Women especially, I believe, are caught in their prayer together between the oppression of a system that will not allow them to choose from among themselves someone who will preside at the ancient rituals of their faith (and that, for dearth of its own ordained ministers, frequently cannot provide them with someone adequate to do it for them), and the need to worship together and to express their togetherness in Christ. In this dilemma it may help to remember that when we gather to pray, not everything needs to be ritualistic. Ritual has its place, but so does quiet gathering.

Prayer that is obedience is listening prayer—the prayer of stillness, of simplicity, of doing and saying nothing, of being with but not of clutching. It is the prayer of "waiting." Though it is true that in many of our prayer services a time of quiet reflection is built in, for many (especially for introverts) the invitation to share, which usually follows this, tends to make the silent period more like rehearsal time for what needs to be said when one's turn comes than one of quiet listening. I wonder what it would be like if religious today gathered more frequently with the express intention of listening; if prior to our congresses or chapter meetings we came together not only to praise, but also to listen for the silent Word of God in our midst speaking to us out of the concrete moment. I do not mean here the time for reflection that many of us provide at moments of communal discernment when all of us can run off into the garden or the chapel to be quiet for a while. I mean *taking time to be alone while being together*, in order to listen to and to experience what John of the Cross calls:

> Silent music,
> Sounding solitude,
> The supper that refreshes, and deepens love.[42]

Prayer that is obedience " is not preoccupied with thought but with the ground of being from which thought takes its origin."[43] It nurtures and prepares us for thought and speech. In it, William Johnson tells us, "lies the true self,"[44] and I would add: In it also can be found depth communion with others. Energy flows through our midst—a sacred presence that lies deep at the core of our togetherness—when we are all gathered to listen. No words can adequately describe this. One moves intensely inward and, the deeper one goes, the more one feels alive, connected to every living being; the more clearly also one opens up in compassion to all the pain in the world.

Healing also happens in our silent solitude-together. It is a healing that is energized from the center where accusations and judgments melt into forgiveness. It is a healing that moves us from our individual and congregational concerns through the pain and suffering of humanity, the agony of the cosmos, into wholeness. No reports can be given of insights gained during our silent time together. No reports need to be given, for the energy will be felt by all and the insights will follow—in God's time.

Obedience That Touches the Universe

The prayer that is obedience needs, of course, be part of us at all times. Our silent moments together remind us of it. This kind of prayer marks our vow as primarily and essentially disposition—an attitude of concernful presence and openness to all things. Our struggles with aging and with diminishment know the depth disposition of obedience with particular acuteness; but so does all authentic movement into maturity and wholeness. The mid-life journey with its yearning for intimacy and gener-

ativity, with its particularly sensitive encounter of the contra-
sexual within, and its need to withdraw projections and face
transference,[45] calls the majority of active religious into a great
deal of patient waiting—into obedience.

A dear friend of mine sees reflected in the agony of our personal journeys the odyssey of all of humankind. Her view may
be particularly helpful in having us understand that the holy
waiting, the patient endurance that is our obedience, is of much
broader significance than merely our personal concerns. We embrace the pain of our journey for the salvation, the conscientization, of all of humankind. The obedience to holistic growth
accepts responsibility for the "Christ" in our title of "Christians." The struggle into maturity, the quest for human integrity,
to which each one of us surrenders out of our own unique sensitivity to the commitment of our vow, has repercussions that
are cosmic in scope. We will recall Gerald May's observations
in the previous chapter concerning the "transmutation of
energy."[46] Though our specific concerns centered there around
the erotic aspects of life-energy, the principle here is the same.
"Agape" energy is the basic life-force of the universe,[47] the
Spirit moving us and all of nature into the fullness we call
Christ. Conscious surrender to this process is what I see first
and foremost as authentic obedience. Through it emerges for us
not just our own personal holiness, but the Christification of the
universe as well. It is, therefore, not just individual in nature but
communal as well, and this in the deepest sense of the word. An
exhortation of Lao Tsu comes to mind; it captures well this disposition of creative releasement that touches the universe:

> Carrying body and soul and embracing the one,
> Can you avoid separation?
> *Attending fully* and becoming supple,
> Can you be as a newborn babe?
> Washing and cleansing the *primal vision,*
> Can you be without stain?
> Loving all . . . and ruling the country,
> *Can you be without cleverness? . . .*
> Understanding and being open to all things,
> Are you able to *do nothing?*
> Giving birth and nourishing,

> Bearing yet not possessing,
> Working yet not taking credit,
> Leading yet not dominating,
> This is the Primal Virtue.[48]

Without attempting to dissect so profound a meditation, we can, nevertheless, quite readily see here poetically expressed much of what we have already touched on: a stress on the incarnational that avoids the temptation of dualism and is open, able to bend and, therefore, ready for new life like a newborn babe. The attentiveness here proposed harkens for the primordial; seeks for depth perception, for original innocence. It loves universally and does not need to be shrewd or to impress with self-sufficiency. It knows the strength of creative passivity and can give and let go. It does not seek praise or power. It leads because it has touched the inner center of all things whence direction flows. It does not need to control because power comes from within.

Authority

With deep sensitivity Lao Tsu blends into harmony for us what in the dualistic tradition has always stood in opposition: listener and leader, obedience and authority. It is clear that in the holistic paradigm only the one who can wait, the listener, who has touched the heart of life and learned from it, can lead. Leadership is never something one "deserves," no matter how hard one has worked or how many committees one has been part of. It worries me in any situation, but particularly in religious life, when elections replace discernment of gifts and when politicking, no matter how pious, enters our leadership process. Subtle as this may be, elections (no matter how democratic they are), because of their affinity with the power play of contemporary politics, too easily lend themselves to a dualistic interpretation of authority. Furthermore, democracy, even at its best, still only displays the "will" of the people. It may have precious little to do with the reign of God.

Religious ought not to win elections. They ought to "experience call." To be sure, this call cannot be purely an external imposition, as most of us experienced it prior to Vatican II and as church structures still foster it, with slight but insignificant modifications, in parish and diocesan settings. The call to leadership emerges out of the recognition within the community that authentic authority is present in an individual and is needed for the growth and wholeness of all. As was mentioned already, inner authority has little to do with "position" ("state"). Discernment within a community, however, does well if it aims at linking the two. This is not, of course, so that, when this happens, we can revert back to seeking all our answers and expecting the solutions to all problems from those "who were chosen to lead us." The word "authority" (Latin: *augere*) means to give increase, to empower, to build up, to edify.[49] As such, authentic authority leads us to the threshold of our own vision and empowers us there. This is what we must come to expect from it. This is what we must seek for in our discernment processes.

The task of authentic authority is primarily to listen to the depth pulsations of the community of which it is a part. Bernard Boelen puts it well when he points out that "mature authority not only has to obey the authority of those who obey, but also has to obey its own authority."[50] It can do this because it knows the meaning of listening and the benefits of waiting; because, on its journey through the dyings and risings of religious life, it has experienced the power of prayer.

On the practical level, "obeying the authority of those who obey" means assuming responsibility for calling the community to be about what we have said we are about, that is, challenging us ever to be who we are. This is by no means always an easy task. It involves, in particular, listening intently to the whole group and differentiating what might be the proclamations of a few possibly strong personalities—perhaps even one's own—from the spirit of the whole. It also demands a blend of compassion and radical honesty. The "kiss" of Dostoyevsky's Jesus is a solemn reminder that autonomous obedience is built on freedom. It is built, however, on honesty as well. The need for approval ought not prevent a leader from saying what must be said. Often timing is of the essence here, of course. The crucifixion of leadership, more often than not, is found in the agony of waiting.

Elsewhere I have suggested that leadership in contemporary times, instead of trying to supply answers, ought much rather model the asking of questions. Its authenticity emerges in its attentive openness to the signs of our time; in its "passionate waiting (with all the pain that this implies) for the questions which radically address us in our age."[51] Its primary mandate is surrender to truth unfolding. Truth, however, reveals itself always as enigmatic. Clarity of personal vision is precisely that, personal. No amount of certainty regarding my own or even a group's correctness will preclude the possibility that someone else's perception may not add something that has simply escaped me (us) and that will, therefore, quite possibly alter the picture. This does not mean, of course, that total indecision is, therefore, inevitable. Decisions, however, and the actions flowing from them are open-ended, not absolute or final. Laws are written in human hearts, not on stone tablets. They are ever respectful of the collective wisdom of the group as it is evolving.

Only when authority closes its eyes to issues at hand, refuses to probe deeper and to ask us to do the same, does indecision and lethargy set in and empowerment cease. Obedience ceases then also and a life dedicated to attentive listening turns into aimless drifting. Instead of challenging ourselves and the way we live to greater authenticity corresponding ever more clearly to our pronounced commitments, we begin rather to move unthinkingly into life-styles of one kind or another only to find ourselves at some point down the line renaming our situations to suit the status quo without ever seeking to know how we got there. An example of this was provided for me not long ago by a young religious deeply concerned with a proposal before the government commission of her congregation. It suggested that, because of the lack of real community among the members, the official name for their living arrangements should be changed from "community" to "local living group," since that more realistically identified what they are. The question here is why matters had been allowed to deteriorate to such an extent and how. What responsibilities had been avoided? Who had neglected the duty of looking into the meaning of community and its challenges; to work toward healing and wholeness among the

various members; to address the issue of indifference and of unhealthy individualism? It may be true that in this case, or in others, very few of us experience the ideal we envision, but can we
with authenticity avoid striving for it and trying to live into its
meaning for us today? What is our vision for religious life today?
What will happen when, because of indifference or thoughtless-
ness, most of us have lost the vision? Who, then, are we?

These are the questions of authentic authority. They rarely are
asked by those who "won the election" by "running a good
campaign" and who may now be too busy maintaining their
popularity to challenge us into authenticity. They are asked only
by those who are obedient to the whole for the sake of the Holy.
These are the poor in spirit who work without "taking credit."
"Understanding and being open to all things," they bear yet do
not possess; they lead yet do not dominate. They practice the
"primal virtue."

Conclusion

I fear that the reading of this reflection on obedience may
prove disappointing to some. In a time when many among us
are struggling with true oppression by the forces of autocracy, it
may not appear helpful to hear about obedience as "surrender to
the depth of one's own integrity." What do we do with actual
oppression that bars some from ministries for arbitrary reasons
and denies dialogue and mutual reflection to others for the sake
of unilateral control? I must sadly confess that I have no answers
here save, once again, the "kiss" of Dostoyevsky's Jesus and the
silence of the man of the Gospel who knew the origin of power
(John 19:11) and was centered there. This did not prevent his
crucifixion, of course (nor does it and will it prevent ours), but
it preserved his integrity, and God raised him up.

As followers of Jesus we must work for God's reign and be
obedient to its mandates. This will at times mean speaking out
against oppression even if we will suffer for it, but, as a community and as individuals, this also means intense discernment lest
we ourselves succumb to the very practice of oppression that we
are called to transform. Our journey depends on our commitment to holiness in our own lives, in our church and in our
world; our integrity lies in our hunger and thirst for justice.

Questions for Focus, Reflection, Discussion

1. How have you experienced authoritarian obedience in your life? How has it affected you? What feelings does this concept evoke? Do you still see it as your major paradigm for obedience? If so, why? If not, why not?

2. "Any kind of interpretation of obedience that refuses to understand culture, history, sociological data, and social responsibility is today simply unconscionable." Is there danger of this in our society? Might we today fall victim too of blindly accepting the status quo? If so, in what areas of our life?

3. How is it that "conditioned blindness" with respect to obedience can lead to lack of self-esteem, self-deprecation? Can you explore practical examples here?

4. What does the statement "Authentic obedience leads toward transformation not preservation," mean to you in your life?

5. Do you see us as communities embracing the trinitarian model of obedience? Has this worked to our advantage or disadvantage? How so?

6. How have you in your life come to understand "obedience for the sake of justice and wholeness"?

7. What is your response to the interpretation of dis-obedience as being "scattered in one's listening, being unwilling or unable to hear the law within"? How does one find the law within? What does it effect in us?

8. What is your reaction to the "crushing of the curse" as part of Christian history to this day, and to the observation that "counter-oppression is oppression also and does not serve our freedom as children of God"?

9. Can obedience, at times, mean dis-obedience? If so, how so? If not, why not? How does this observation relate to the insight that "freedom without obedience is not freedom. It is license instead"?

10. "The power of authentic obedience lies first and foremost in the depth and surrender of the human heart sensitized by patient endurance." Have you experienced this?

11. How is it that depth obedience is the unifying force for all three vows? Do you agree with this insight?

12. Have you ever experienced "silent solitude-together"? If so, was it effective for community discernment? Did it bring about healing?

13. What is your response to the observation that the agony of our personal journey reflects the odyssey of all humankind; our struggle into maturity, our quest for integrity has cosmic repercussions?

14. —"Only the listener who has touched the heart of life and learned from it, can lead."

—"Leadership is never something a person deserves."

—"Religious ought not to *win* elections. They ought to *experience call.*"

—"The call to leadership emerges out of the recognition within the community that authentic authority is present in an individual and is needed for the growth and wholeness of all."

—"Authentic authority leads us to the threshold of our own vision and empowers us there."

—"Mature authority not only has to obey the authority of those who obey, but also has to obey its own authority."

—"Authority needs to be about challenging us ever to be who we are."

What do these statements mean to you? Have you experienced leadership that way?

6

Conversion toward Increase

We began our reflection on living the vows in today's world with a story: the message of the rainmaker of Kiaochau. Stories can be powerful change agents. Once we have heard them, they have a tendency to stay with us; to accompany us and to call us back to themselves whenever the need arises in order to help draw us in from being too scattered, from being lost in "outwardness"—at the circle's rim. We can dwell in stories. They neither force us to concentrate unnecessarily, nor rush us. They capture us instead and fascinate. Joseph Campbell, reflecting on Jung's respect for stories and myths, tells us that when we are too outward oriented and have lost touch with our inner energies, myths and stories are the means of bringing us back in touch with ourselves. "They are telling us in picture language of powers of the psyche to be recognized and integrated in our lives, powers that have been common to the human spirit forever, and which represent that wisdom of the species by which [we have] weathered the millenniums."[1] If we take stories seriously and dialogue with them we can learn much and "come to terms with the greater horizon of our own deeper and wiser, inward self."[2] Good stories tell truths but rarely threaten or frighten us. Jesus used stories, we know, as his most successful way of teaching, because stories bring us home to our own integrity. John Shea claims that for Christians, ever since Jesus, the perennial strategy has been to "1. Gather folks. 2. Break bread. 3. Tell the stories."[3] This has worked so well because story

telling has, in fact, been an addiction for humans since the beginning of creation. "No matter our mood, in reverie or expec-
tation, panic or peace, we can be found stringing together
incidents, and unfolding episodes. We turn our pain into narrative so we can bear it; we turn our ecstasy into narrative so we
can prolong it. We all seem to be under the sentence of Scheher-
azade. *We tell our stories to live.*"[4]

And so it seems fitting to begin these considerations—concerned with the possibility of new life in religious congregations
today, but also shadowed by the very real possibility of death—
with just one more story. It is a story with which many of us
may already be acquainted.[5] Like all good stories, it has universal significance. In my sharing it here, however, I want to claim
it specifically as ours, for it speaks very sensitively to the whole
picture: the pain, the discouragement, the yearning, the sharing,
the hope, and the promise that is religious life today. It is a story
about grace and about the responsibility with which grace always gifts us. It is a story about silence, about wonder, about
reverence, about trust, and ultimately about new life:

There was a famous monastery which had fallen on very hard times.
Formerly its many buildings were filled with young monks and its big
church resounded with the singing of the chant, but now it was de-
serted. People no longer came there to be nourished by prayer. A
handful of old monks shuffled through the cloisters and praised their
God with heavy hearts.

On the edge of the monastery woods, an old rabbi had built a little
hut. He would come there from time to time to fast and pray. No one
ever spoke with him, but whenever he appeared, the word would be
passed from monk to monk: "The rabbi walks in the woods." And, for
as long as he was there, the monks would feel sustained by his prayerful presence.

One day the abbot decided to visit the rabbi and to open his heart to
him. So, after the morning Eucharist, he set out through the woods.
As he approached the hut, the abbot saw the rabbi standing in the
doorway, his arms outstretched in welcome. It was as though he had
been waiting there for some time. The two embraced like long-lost
brothers. Then they stepped back and just stood there, smiling at one
another with smiles their faces could hardly contain.

After a while the rabbi motioned the abbot to enter. In the middle of the room was a wooden table with the Scriptures open on it. They sat there for a moment, in the presence of the book. Then the rabbi began to cry. The abbot could not contain himself. He covered his face with his hands and began to cry too. For the first time in his life, he cried his heart out. The two men sat there like two lost children, filling the hut with their sobs and wetting the wood of the table with their tears.

After the tears had ceased to flow and all was quiet again, the rabbi lifted his head. "You and your brothers are serving God with heavy hearts," he said. "You have come to ask a teaching of me. I will give you a teaching, but you can only repeat it once. After that, no one must ever say it aloud again."

The rabbi looked straight at the abbot and said, "The Messiah is among you."

For a while, all was silent. Then the rabbi said, "Now you must go."

The abbot left without a word and without ever looking back.

The next morning, the abbot called his monks together in the chapter room. He told them that he had received a teaching from "the rabbi who walks in the woods" and that this teaching was never again to be spoken aloud. Then he looked at each of his brothers and said, "The rabbi said that one of us is the Messiah."

The monks were startled by this saying. "What could it mean?" they asked themselves. "Is Brother John the Messiah? Or Father Matthew? Or Brother Thomas? Am I the Messiah? What could this mean?"

They were all deeply puzzled by the rabbi's teaching. But no one ever mentioned it again.

As time went by, the monks began to treat one another with a very special reverence. There was a gentle, wholehearted, human quality about them now which was hard to describe but easy to notice. They lived with one another as men who had finally found something. But they prayed the Scriptures together as men who were always looking for something. Occasional visitors found themselves deeply moved by the life of these monks. Before long, people were coming from far and wide to be nourished by the prayer life of the monks and young men were asking, once again, to become part of the community.

In those days, the rabbi no longer walked the woods. His hut had fallen into ruins. But, somehow or other, the old monks who had taken his teaching to heart still felt sustained by his prayerful presence.

We tell stories to live. Perhaps no other concern haunts religious today more than the question of declining life in their congregations and the future of religious life. Somehow what we are about receives encouragement when we know that others are joining us around the same effort; that we are not alone. There is a sense of worthwhileness that is enhanced when new membership gathers around us because of our mission. It is difficult to experience diminishment, death, and painful to question into it and to ask "why." Teilhard de Chardin speaks of the diminishment of physical death with great insight:

God must, in some way or other, make room for Himself [Herself], hollowing us out and emptying us, if [S/He] is finally to penetrate into us. And in order to assimilate us in Him [Her], [S/He] must break the molecules of our being so as to re-cast and re-model us. The function of death is to provide the necessary entrance into our inmost selves.[6]

Perhaps religious congregations today are experiencing this necessary "hollowing out," this emptying that will ultimately make room for God. It may be disconcerting for some of us even to conceive, let alone admit, that institutions expressly formed for the consecrated life need "hollowing out." Yet perhaps this is where our questioning will lead us. Death, says de Chardin, "will put us into the state organically needed if the divine fire is to descend upon us.[7]

I have already pointed out, and students of human development assure us, that the maturation process of the human person passes through a number of deaths and resurrections—crises— that can quite readily be paralleled with the turning points of cultures and systems as they move toward their own fulfillment. What is characteristic of every crisis or turning point is the death or disintegration of the dominant mode of perception that is always necessary before anything new can appear. In chapter 1 I discussed the natural resistance to this letting go and the danger of intransigence and the subsequent "calcification" of one's mode of seeing and behaving into which one can slip in order to avoid the pain of death.

It is natural for persons in crisis situations to pass through prolonged periods of desolation and darkness after the initial experience of death. For individuals this period may consist of several years. A culture, however, paralleling this experience, may need to endure it for decades or even centuries. Institutions such as ours may be in transition for a very long time also for, as I suggested already, we are inextricably connected with the movements and processes of our time. During these periods one (the individual with respect to his or her own life, as well as with respect to institutions and cultures) experiences the previous, comfortable mode of perception and behavior to have disintegrated completely, but nothing as yet has taken its place. One feels oneself in absolute darkness, in the desert of utter need, an ocean of nothingness with no direction to follow: no past to revert back to, no future to hope for. The great temptation during such times is to give up instead of learning from the signs of the times; to despair and to make decisions accordingly. By this, however, one forces the process into one's own direction and runs the risk of aborting it. The silent waiting of the rainmaker and the prayer of the "rabbi who walked in the woods" alone prepare the way of redemption.

And when redemption comes, it rarely does so with great noise and tumultuous change. Perhaps this is the paradox of it all. During a silent night in Bethlehem a child was born and only the poor noticed. Cannons and swords can bring about change but rarely effect transformation. A little babe in swaddling clothes and, later, a silent carpenter for thirty-some years held within himself the energy that would forever alter perception and make all things new.

It is interesting to note what happened to the old monks "with heavy hearts" after the rabbi's message was imparted to them. The story tells us that they were startled, that they wondered, but that they never mentioned it again. Like Mary, they kept these things each one in his heart. They let their hearts teach them and slowly their vision was transformed: "They began to treat each other with a very special reverence" which was "easy to notice," but hard to describe or talk about and had certainly never been programed or planned. People were attracted to them once again because they prayed with longing and lived lives filled with purpose: *The Messiah was in their midst.*

We have here a very powerful message for ourselves and our future. Since Vatican II we have spent a great deal of energy and talent addressing the vocation issue. Almost no other program in religious life has received equal attention, planning, discussion, and worry; almost no other program has been revised and rediscerned as frequently as "formation." Yet our houses remain empty and the talented people we train for "formation" all seem underemployed. Why is this so? Are we perhaps, in spite of our good intentions, asking the wrong questions, having out-dated expectations, making unrealistic demands? Are we truly moving into the center of this issue, or are we in fact staying dangerously close to the rim, forever spending our energies at reforming our programs instead of surrendering our hearts to the rabbi's message and allowing *ourselves* to be transformed?

Expectations and Assumptions

Some time ago a student of mine in the lay ministry training program with which I am associated informed me that she was putting her house up for rent and moving in with a local community of women religious to live with them a life of simplicity and to share community. She is a mother of several grown children, divorced, has worked for a number of years, and now feels a call to simplify her life, and a desire to experience the companionship of other women working in various and diverse ministries in the church.

Needless to say, I was pleased with her decision; fascinated particularly by the fact that she had really no immediate interest in joining the community as a vowed member, but simply wanted to live with and share, to com-panion—"break bread with." Her story led me to reflect about new movements in religious life, new avenues of response to the vocation crisis, new life in the midst of apparent death. It led me also to probe into the kind of expectations we continue to have; the demands we continue to make.

To begin with, it is clear to anyone who takes the trouble to observe that our newer members, though small in numbers, show great diversity with respect to almost every aspect of their lives. Age, life and ministry background, interests, education, relational experiences, culture, and race can all be quite different for each. Furthermore, few religious congregations still accept young girls or boys into their "formation" programs, so that persons discerning a religious vocation for the most part tend to be at least young to middle adults if not older. (The oldest "newer" member I ever taught in the Studies of Spirituality Program designed for them, was seventy-two years old.) We expect them to behave according to their age. Our philosophy is, and rightly so, that they need to have navigated at least the major phases of adolescence in order to appreciate the implications of religious commitment. We hope that they will have experienced life, dated, worked, become professionally competent, self-directed, responsible.

What continues to puzzle me, however, is why, in spite of our awareness of all this and our well-grounded policies concerning the admittance of candidates, our response to the women and men who come to explore our life-style continues to seem out of touch and obsolete in many instances. If the men and women coming to us are indeed as mature as our policies expect them to be, why do we not treat them that way? Why do our assumptions, in fact, appear in many cases to be still those of years ago? If these women and men, on the other hand, are not as mature as our policies expect them to be, why do we encourage them toward incorporation in the first place?

A member of the leadership team of a large religious congregation recently shared with me her puzzlement at the fact that newer members were being attracted but somehow, after a period of investigation, did not stay. "We draw them, but we cannot seem to keep them," she said. The reasons for this can, of course, be many and in some instances there may even be a "lack of vocation." However, could one of the reasons not be our expectations and demands of them once they enter—demands, I might add, which few of us live up to ourselves?

What, for example, is the meaning of restricting adults to sleeping in designated "novitiate houses" for an exact number of days during the canonical year, in order to fulfill canon law requirements? If ever the maxim that "the law is made for humans, not humans for the law" should be applied, this certainly is the case. I know of a grown woman who had to cut short an important family reunion meeting because her specific number of days "outside the nest" had run out. What is the point of this and what the witness value? Why, to give an example perhaps less extreme and, therefore, also more prevalent, do we often expect "novices" to be poorer than we are? If, for example, our newer members need transportation, why are there still instances when they are told to take the bus while the rest of us drive cars for lesser distances? Why are their budgets in some congregations smaller than those of the "professed" and frequently determined by someone else? Why must they lose weight to make the right impression "novices" ought to make, while the rest of us are forever breaking our diets? Why must they be evaluated (often by us) while our behavior goes unaddressed? I am not suggesting that all requirements are unreasonable. I am merely claiming that we must practice what we preach and cannot blindly follow a double standard without serious consequences. The days of "segregated novitiates" are over. Adults notice inconsistencies and are not edified by them.

Time, Trust, and Freedom

It is clear that no woman in America *needs* to enter religious life today to improve her status. Men who see ordained ministry as a status symbol may still on occasion seek entrance into religious community to obtain orders. But generally men do not *need* to enter community to improve their status either. Education and advancement in the professional sphere are now open to all women alike and certainly to men. I do not by that fact imply that improvement for all women and for minorities is not warranted regarding this issue in society at large, but only wish to make the point that membership in a religious community will certainly not bring this about for anyone. Men and woman who enter, therefore, in America at least or in other countries of similar economic standing, do not seem to do so for social status. And, as I have mentioned already, although they will identify ministry as one of the major reasons for coming,[8] it is not their prior incompetence in ministry and consequent need for training by religious, but rather their desire to *minister together with others* joined in a common cause (a community) that has them seek out religious life.

Those who come to join us also do not as a whole need training in the social etiquette requisite for a professional, that is, proper manners and general demeanor. They are not ignorant (in need of advice from any and all "older" professed). Frequently they do not require ministry discernment either and will not necessarily need to be exposed to every single ministerial option the congregation can offer them. Many of them have their ministry already chosen and, if not, are quite capable of looking around for themselves, of exploring, asking questions. They, more often than not, can on their own, without preprogramed "mini-ministry experiences," seek the opportunities they need for discernment, provided these are offered them, as they are in fact offered to most of us, through our ministry offices. They are, after all, adults, and it is on that premise that we have invited them to be with us. Mature adults naturally ask questions when they need information and resist problems being solved for them. They find it difficult to be given answers to questions they have not even asked yet.

Once again, I am not suggesting that the men and women coming to discern religious life will not need advice and help. I am merely proposing that we will need to respect their right to seek it, and allow them the opportunity to do so in their own time. The Messiah is among them too. Rushing their insight, no matter how sure we are of what is "good for them," only violates the process of emergence. That this may be frustrating for some of us goes without saying. The difference between the functional mode of dealing with persons that springs from dualism and the personal way of relating with others that evolves from the holistic attitude discussed in chapter 1, is precisely in our ability to wait and to let be. It seems to me that some of the greatest frustration points in our life together as a community generally lie precisely in our attempts to "make each other over" into our own image and likeness. The hardest part of living together for many of us, and perhaps one of the main reasons why we ought to invest quality time in getting to know one another, is learning to "let be" and trusting enough to "let God," without, however, sinking into indifference. There is a fine balance here between concern and control, and one that needs particular attention in our interactions with newer members.

The Stress Factor

My seven years of experience with newer members leave me no doubt that much of the unhappiness they experience in their initial years of religious life revolves around control issues as well as policies requiring frequent mobility. Having already experienced one major stress factor in the life-change they have chosen to make, it is of little help to them that so many congregations propose numerous changes in living situations and ministerial explorations during their discernment years. This, furthermore, is of questionable value from the perspective of community discernment as well. Too much change and excessive control, besides preventing any possibility for establishing meaningful relationships, tend to bring out regressive tendencies in even the healthiest adult. Hence, if some of our newer members seem to exhibit "dysfunctional relational patterns" (as one "formation" team pointed out to me), or discover within themselves problems with authority, sexuality and, sometimes, chemical dependency, the stress we often put them under by overplanning their lives and moving them from one "formation" site to another* can certainly be counted as a contributing factor.

Dr. Jackie Schwartz, management consultant and family therapist, in her work *Letting Go of Stress* cites stress factors conducive to illness. Among them I counted a significant number applicable to persons entering religious life. Not the least of these are changes of residence, major changes in social activities, changing to a different line of work, changes in responsibility at work, changes in living conditions (group living, climate), revisions of personal habits (dress, manners, personal associations, cultural expectations, diet), changes in the number of family get-togethers, and others.[9] Citing the Lisa F. Berkman and S. Leonard Syme nine-year study on stress, Schwartz emphasizes the need for an adequate support system to maintain good health:

*Even as I was writing this, one of the newer members of a major international congregation told me that during the last eight years of her initial "formation" she had to pack and move eighteen times. She feels that she has come close to losing any desire for community involvement, all energy for forming relationships or working on confrontation. There simply never was enough time to get to know anyone deeply enough.

Every time I found evidence of disrupted social relationships, I found evidence of some sort of negative health outcome. And the range of disease outcomes is very broad indeed. For example, people with interrupted social ties exhibit more depression, unhappiness, and loss of morale . . . higher morbidity rates for such illnesses as gastrointestinal upset, skin problems, arthritis, and headaches.[10]

A large number of symptoms indicating excessive amounts of stress can be detected among many of our newer members. Besides the general irritability, hyperexcitation or depression so frequently present, one often can observe impulsive behavior, emotional instability, the overpowering urge to cry, the loss of joie de vivre with which they came, emotional tension, high-pitched laughter, hypermotility, loss of appetite or overeating, increased smoking, and even at times, increased use of legal drugs, alcohol, and other substance abuse.[11] The danger of misdiagnosing stress-related symptoms as indicative of problems in the personality of the newer member is clear. Instead of addressing the cause of the stress, reducing stress factors wherever possible, and arranging programs of initiation to suit the demands and needs of the times, as well as of the individual, we often place the onus entirely on newer members and question their capacity for adjustment to situations that may be entirely unnecessary and totally unrelated to the essentials of discernment.

It may be that for many of us stress is one of those things one grins and bears. To introduce it here as a significant factor to be taken seriously in the discernment of vocation may strike some as an exaggeration, even "sissification" of the process. *We* had no such consideration. Yet, true as this is, many of us are also here to manifest the consequences of such neglect. Perhaps a greater sensitivity to stress-related dysfunctionality could raise our own levels of compassion both for ourselves and others, and enhance our living together considerably. As Richard M. Stein points out: "Stress has been studied objectively by scientists for less than forty years. In that same period of time, the ramifications of modern technology have contributed new sources of stimuli and stress which were unimaginable when the scientific study began."[12] We live in times of change. We need to take these times seriously if we wish to be viable witnesses of God's compassion and mercy.

Drawn to Prayer and to Community

It seems reasonable to propose that contemporary men and women seeking religious life are also persons attracted to prayer and community. Being adult, many of them were probably drawn by someone among us with whom they have shared prayer and with whom they have interacted on a personal level previously. When they come to us, therefore, many of our newer members already pray and commune. Like us, however, they cannot pray with everyone equally well and, because of the theological divergence in community generally, they can perhaps not pray with some sisters or brothers at all; but, then, neither can we. Like us they will want to look for a compatible local community. Their education, background, interests, needs cannot be satisfied equally well in all of our communities, nor should our "training" of them demand this. In fact, I wonder whether, within the holistic paradigm we are called to embrace today, we ought to "train" anyone. The entire notion of "formation" is Aristotelian-Thomistic at best and does not speak of our contemporary understanding of person, which resists "mold" and "form" and honors the emergence of inner capacities and strengths, given proper environment and empowerment. The term "novitiate" also seems questionable and I find it disrespectful of the adults we hope to attract. Etymologically it refers to the "uninitiated," those in need of guidance and "training," not to men and women seeking a community of adults for adults as adults; not to mature persons drawn to community because of an inner sense of call to minister with, to pray with, to share.

It is my sincere conviction that the women and men who want to walk with us and break bread with us in religious life today do not need "formation." Like us, they will need and they will ask for spiritual direction and guidance. They will request it of those among us or elsewhere who will inspire them and empower them toward further growth. They may not always ask it of their "formation" directors. The policy of receiving spiritual direction from someone whom the system, as it prevails to date, still sees as primarily responsible for assessment and evaluation is administratively "unclean" and can be psychologically, as well as spiritually, damaging. It opens up the possibility for mistrust and even dishonesty.

Like any other adult, the men and women drawn to community will need to be able to discern the place and the group with whom this community can be experienced. It is clear that being new, they will need our help and suggestions in doing this, and the communities involved need to dialogue and discern as well. What no one today needs, however, is the orchestrated environment of a community set apart for "formation." It may be true that few of our present community situations are ideal. That, I am sure, needs to be addressed and cannot be avoided while we propose band-aid solutions to "formation" problems. Those coming to discern their call to religious life are coming to join *us*. They are seeking an active, ongoing life-style of ministry and community. They are looking to meet the women and men with whom they will spend their lives. They do not need a preprogramed package of what they may never experience after they have taken their vows. If we cannot meet them where we live and as we live, perhaps we should not encourage them to come.

Nor does the rationale of having all newer members live together for purposes of bonding hold up anymore. To begin with, few religious congregations experience that great an influx of newer members that a viable community situation can be formed for any stable length of time to enable bonding and relationship in a realistic sense of the word. Secondly, the individuals coming may quite possibly come from diverse areas of the country; from diverse cultures. They may vary greatly in age and interest. To assume that, because they are all new in the congregation, they will automatically bond with each other and form the "support system," the "band," we all had, is to look for something that may no longer be real for them. They should not be asked to live community without, like us, being part of discerning its direction and composition. They should not be asked to live community at any cost, in any setting, especially a prearranged one. In other words, they should not at any time be expected, as they so often are even today, to "grin and bear it."

Unless an adult model of interaction is encouraged right from the start, adult behavior cannot be expected. This can, of course, be a considerable challenge for us as we struggle with the very real community issues discussed in chapter 4. Facing the question of new membership in the midst of our own acknowledged brokenness is indeed difficult, but it can no longer be swept aside or passed on to a few "well trained directors of formation." If we want increase, we (all of us) will have to surrender to the conversion that is asked of us. This means opening not only our houses but also our hearts to those who seek incorporation. They will not forever knock at the doors of our already existing friendships to seek inclusion. They yearn to live with, be with, suffer and celebrate with us, to work out their journey with its history, its brokenness, and its future with us, and to be there for us in our journey as well. But they cannot be asked to do this in the vacuum left after we go off to be involved with our well-established relationships weekend after weekend; night after night. We need to include them into the reality of our communities and our lives. We have no ivory-tower setting to offer them. Our reality needs to be offered honestly: a group of struggling, loving women and men who invite them into their midst to join in the journey home; to minister and be ministered to; to help and be helped.

As I mentioned already, the men and women who come to join us these days are very much products of this age. They will want to experience with us in diverse ways how to be effectively lovers of God's *basileia*. The countercultural stance of celibate loving may be new to many of them. We can share our dreams, our visions with them. They, on the other hand, may bring new energy, new hope to tired hearts. Their life-experiences—very different from ours, especially if we entered young—can be of great value to us. Their style of communicating, of confrontation and interaction, may be very helpful for our explorations into new forms of relating and being with one another. We might learn much from them, not only from their experiences, but also about us: about our charism, about our willingness to learn, as well as our willingness to share. In turn, we invite them to learn. They are invited, not programed. Our interaction with them ought to be mutual and open ended. We invite them to move with us in shared responsibility toward our charism— the Christian message particularized in our communal setting. Their communion with us flows from our already existing communities. It is not forced in stereotyped group sessions with other "young professed" on programed weekends or at study days that they all "must" attend because *we* feel it is good for them.

Organic Incorporation

Adults today, if they respond in an adult way to an adult congregation, may wish to commit themselves in varying degrees: for several years, for one year at a time, forever, or simply as associate members. In the latter form there may be many variations, ranging from live-in associates to prayer associates. They may wish to be ministerially bonded only, or may wish to be communally bonded but work in what some congregations may still regard as "secular" professions. Their discernment with us in all this should be open-ended and dialogical, in the spirit of mature interrelationship where the needs of all are considered and respected.

Incorporation that is oriented to diversity must be "organic" rather than "institutional." By this I mean a "being drawn" that is natural rather than formal: adults attracted to a particular local group get invited in or ask to live with them. In that group they pray, commune, share of their resources, and discern membership even while membership is going on. They move into the larger group as the spirit directs: slowly, through visits to the provincial house, congresses, assemblies, and the like. They reach beyond the local community when the need presents itself and shared discernment directs it. The community, including all its members, evaluates the situation of that community, not only of the new member. There is a general recognition that the Spirit gifts each member with various insights concerning the whole.

Organic incorporation means that the women or men interested in our life-style are simply invited to be the women or men *they* are, among the women or men *we* are, with all the risks that growing together implies. They, no doubt, will want and need a contact sister or brother: someone who walks with them and can share our history with them. The congregation will need someone trained in coordinating the various modes of membership, to make resources available and give support. Most of all we will need community-life facilitators: those who are trained to help local communities in their personal interactions, conflicts, goal setting, and evaluations. We will need them to help all of us become aware of the demands of intimacy that are beginning to emerge among us now that our relatively professional way of handling diversified ministries has moved us past our identity crises into the need for depth relation and generativity.

We all know that there is enough neurosis and dysfunctionality in our midst; that we do not need a new influx. In order to prevent this, the vision of organic incorporation I suggest here will need much thought and prayer. But it will also need generosity and the willingness to risk. It will certainly not guard us against mistakes but, then, neither has the model of "formation" most congregations have followed up to now.

I have experienced both excitement and resistance to this possibly new vision toward increase when I have presented it to various groups. The excitement frequently came from the men and women now in "formation," but also from those who knew interested persons but saw them as too mature for the structures of incorporation presently in use in most religious communities. They found themselves hesitant to recommend sometimes even their own congregations to these individuals. Positive response has often come also from religious working in areas away from the motherhouse; away from large numbers of their own congregation. For them, associate membership with other women and men is part of their own support system. They treasure these mature interactions and would welcome more organic ways of connecting their friends with their congregations.

Among the negative reactions, mistrust in one's own ability to deal with newer members and a desire to leave this to the experts is certainly one. Some have pointed out to me that newer members are not always as mature as I seem to imply. I hasten to point out that neither are we, and that the maturity we are striving for is there to be aspired to by all of us. The organic approach is unquestionably one of risk. It disrupts old, well oiled methods designed for step-by-step progress and eventual closure to a process of incorporation. It can, therefore, make us very nervous for, among other things, it will not provide us with the certainty of a "job well done." Thus it is quite probable, for example, that knowledge of the vows will be difficult to measure when discernment is individualized and spans over years; when the "religious" emerges out of each newer member slowly, and stamps the congregation each time with originality. It may be difficult and at times disconcerting for some of us to experience in the lived reality of our newer members that vows are not once and for all entities that we "take," at a fixed moment in time, forever. We may commit ourselves forever, but the substance of our commitment deepens and may in a very real sense change as life teaches us the reality of our promise. This, I have suggested throughout these pages, is true for all of us, not just for our newer members. When one is "formed" in a dualistic paradigm, however, as many of us were before Vatican II, expectations of closure and measurability die hard. It is difficult to accept that few if any of us know fully what we vow when we vow it; that our commitment is surrender to the mystery; that, organically speaking, having only a glimpse is really all that can be expected even on the day of final profession.

We spend most of our lives living into the vowed experience, altering our motivations frequently; hopefully ever toward greater depth. We are all "a risk." The intensity of the vowed experience lies ever in the yearning. Knowledge, as well as the ability to articulate, is really secondary. To feel this yearning in all humility is grace; to speak about it, on the other hand, may be one of the riskiest attempts of all. I know, therefore, that moving into "organic" modes of incorporation is easier suggested than carried out. To feel the necessity for it within us is one thing; sensitively to witness it unfolding in our newer members may be quite another. It requires above all compassionate being-with, patience, sisterly and brotherly love, which, more than anything else, knows the power of releasement. It requires persistent obedience to one's own integrity. It requires the knowledge of the "rabbi who walked in the woods."

What we have to offer is precious but, like all things precious, it must be handled gently in open hands and with hospitality and trust, out of a sense of sharing rather than bestowing, or else it will be broken or lost. Our trust and hospitality, no doubt, will bring us suffering as it did to our founders, but it brought holiness (wholeness) as well. It brought women and men of vision; it brought increase.

Questions for Focus, Reflection, Discussion

1. "We tell our stories to live." How does the rabbi's message gift religious congregations with life?

2. Does Teihard de Chardin's meditation on death have significance for religious life as you see it? Do we as congregations need to be "hollowed out" to make room for God?

3. Do you experience resistance to the letting-go required for the sake of new life? Are we as congregations realistically facing the possibility of death? Are we in the "desert of need"?

4. What is your attitude toward and what are your expectations of the newer members of your congregation? Are you willing to share your life with them in community?

5. What, do you think, are the reasons why "we draw them but cannot seem to keep them"?

6. What does religious life have to offer today? Why would a man or woman want to join your congregation? What model of life would you like to live and would you propose for our newer members?

7. Do you agree that "some of the greatest frustration points in our life together as a community generally lie in our attempts to 'make each other over' into our own image and likeness"? Does this apply to our attitude toward our newer members as well?

8. What is the difference between "letting-be" in order to "let God," and indifference?

9. Can you identify stress factors in the life of our newer members? What do you see as the solution to the seemingly excessive amounts of stress experienced by them?

10. "If we want increase, we (all of us) will have to surrender to the conversion that is asked of us. This means opening not only our houses but also our hearts to those who seek incorporation." What is your reaction to this observation?

11. How do you respond to the varied ways of membership suggested in this chapter? How has your congregation acted in this area up to now?

12. What would you add to this chapter's reflection on "organic" incorporation? How practical is it? How risky? Is it worth trying?

Epilogue

Just as I was nearing the end of writing these reflections a list of questions and concerns was sent to me by members of a major religious congregation in order to help me prepare an address for their yearly assembly. Among these there are several, I believe, that are particularly important for us today:

—I believe religious life is dead—community as we have lived it and as we continue to try to live it and structure it, does not work. Can we start talking about this and come to a point of shaping the future rather than have it shape us by default?
—When will we get to the point of discussing our vision of the future without fear?
—Why do we stay in religious life? What are our dreams? How are we together in community?
—Our first concern needs to be how we *live* together and how we *are* together.

These issues are not new for any of us. Some of us hold them quietly in our hearts; others, more boldly, want them addressed at yearly assemblies; all of us ask them. There is much sadness in many of these questions; sometimes even desperation. They are the questions of the "turning point"—the crisis of our way of life and, although solutions to the difficulties they raise will probably never come by way of clear-cut formulas or constitutional reformulation (many of us have spent hours already in vain trying to make this happen), in a certain sense, and encouragingly so, an answer to them is already emerging *in the very asking of the question.* Awareness and recognition—the intentional exposure of oneself to the darkness and (as the rainmaker did) to

157

the "drought," in spite of the pain that this involves—is the beginning of vision.

We will remember, however, that that vision when it emerges will not be our achievement. (The rainmaker did not do anything. He merely surrendered to the Tao.) True vision always is a gift. When it graces us, therefore, we do not experience "sight" as much as we experience "being sighted," being drawn, being enticed into depth. Our answers, then, will emerge out of that depth. The struggle with formulas, decrees, and properly stated resolutions concerning our life and our mission, important though these may be, will be quite secondary, for our actions will flow from an inner encounter with our deepest self and, through it, with all of humankind.

For the activists among us the invitation to creative waiting, to quiet watchfulness and passionate surrender, may seem quite useless. None of what I have suggested, however, implies inaction or quietism. When Paul pointed out to the Romans that hoping "for what we cannot see means awaiting it with patient endurance"(Rom. 8:25), he was not recommending passivity, but merely exhorting them to recognize their own limits as they work toward establishing God's reign; to give heed and to surrender to a greater power. The invitation given by Rahner and cited in chapter 2 comes to mind:

Give . . . deeper realities of the spirit a chance now to rise to the surface: silence, fear, the ineffable longing for truth, for love, for fellowship, for God. Face loneliness, fear, imminent death! Allow such ultimate, basic human experiences to come first. *Don't go talking about them, making up theories about them, but simply endure these basic experiences.*[1]

Religious life today finds itself in crisis. The time has come, therefore, to draw inward together and alone, to embrace the depth questions of our vowed life and to put ourselves "back in the Tao," so that the rain may once again come. Before we do any more, we need to be: to face and endure the darkness. The preceding pages have attempted to help us in this; to open up the issues and suggest possibilities without attempting to give solutions; to invite all of us to keep asking, to keep exploring, to keep risking. Crises, as we know, are not solved. They resolve themselves in their own time, in God's time. Ours is ever the task of obedient listening even as we wait passionately and creatively for "the grace of a better dawn" (M. Heidegger).

Notes

Chapter 1/Turning Point

1. Jean Shinoda Bolen, M.D., *The Tao of Psychology* (San Francisco: Harper & Row, 1982), p. 98.
2. Fritjof Capra, *The Turning Point* (New York: Simon and Schuster, 1982), pp. 15–16.
3. Ibid., p. 28.
4. Ibid., p. 26.
5. Martin Heidegger, *Vorträge und Aufsätze*, 3 vols., 3rd ed. (Pfullingen: Günther Neske, 1967), 1:28 (trans. mine).
6. Capra, p. 16.
7. Edward C. Whitmont, *Return of the Goddess* (New York: Crossroad, 1984), p. 125.
8. Joann Wolski Conn, ed., *Women's Spirituality: Resources for Christian Development* (New York: Paulist Press, 1986), p. 49.
9. Hence the emphasis among spiritual writers on breathing and posture in relation to prayer. The panting, hurried breather says much about life and his or her attitude—conscious or not—toward ultimate concerns.
10. Wolski Conn, p. 50.
11. Ibid., p. 51.
12. Beatrice Bruteau, "Neo-Feminism and the Next Revolution of Consciousness," *Anima* 3/2 (Spring 1977): 1.
13. Whitmont, p. 124.
14. Sandra Schneiders, *Women and the Word* (New York: Paulist Press, 1986), p. 19 (italics mine).
15. Bernard J. Boelen, *Personal Maturity* (New York: Seabury Press, 1978), p. 79.
16. John Shea, *Stories of God* (Chicago: Thomas More Press, 1978), front cover and p. 39.
17. Elisabeth Schüssler Fiorenza, *In Memory of Her* (New York: Crossroad, 1984), p. 113.
18. Ibid., pp. 119–20.
19. Ibid.

20. Edward Schillebeeckx, *On Christian Faith* (New York: Crossroad, 1987), p. 17.

21. Ibid., p. 18.

22. Schüssler Fiorenza, p. 121.

23. Schneiders, pp. 41–50.

24. Ibid., p. 45.

25. Schüssler Fiorenza, chap. 5.

26. Joseph S. O'Leary, *Questioning Back* (Minneapolis: Winston Press, 1985), p. 152.

27. Ibid., pp. 152–53.

28. Ibid., p. 176.

29. Ibid.

30. Ibid., p. 177.

31. Ibid.

32. James J. Bacik, *Apologetics and the Eclipse of Mystery* (Notre Dame, Ind.: Notre Dame University Press, 1980), p. 3.

33. Capra, p. 76.

34. Cited by Aniela Jaffé, *The Myth of Meaning* (New York: Penguin, 1975), p. 35.

35. Cited by ibid., p. 31.

36. Matthew Fox, *Meditations with Meister Eckhart* (Santa Fe: Bear & Co., 1982), pp. 16, 18, 32–33.

37. Gabriele Uhlheim, *Meditations with Hildegard of Bingen* (Santa Fe: Bear & Co., 1982), pp. 32, 34, 35.

38. Cited by George A. Maloney, S.J., *God's Exploding Love* (New York: Alba House, 1987), pp. 23–24.

39. Fox, pp. 22–23.

40. Barbara Fiand, *Releasement* (New York: Crossroad, 1987), pp. 78–79.

41. O'Leary, p. 176.

42. Fiand, p. 5.

43. Matthew Fox, *Breakthrough* (Garden City, N.Y.: Image Books, 1980), p. 103.

44. Ibid., p. 67.

45. Ibid., p. 59.

46. Sue Woodruff, *Meditations with Mechtild of Magdeburg* (Santa Fe: Bear & Co., 1982), pp. 13–14.

47. Ibid., p. 15.

48. Fox, *Meditations*, p. 82.

49. Bernhard Welte, *Meister Eckhart* (Freiburg: Herder, 1979), p. 134.

50. Karl Rahner S.J., *Theological Investigations*, vol. 1, trans. Cornelius Ernst O.P. (London: Darton, Longman & Todd, 1965), p. 310.

51. Karl Rahner, *Theological Investigations,* vol. 6, trans. Karl-H. and Boniface Kruger (New York: Crossroad, 1974), pp. 393–94.

52. Roger Haight, S.J., *The Experience and Language of Grace* (New York: Paulist Press, 1979), p. 128.

53. Fox, *Meditations,* p. 86.

54. Schüssler Fiorenza, p. 135.

55. Fox, *Meditations,* p. 102.

56. Schüssler Fiorenza, p. 130.

57. Ibid., p. 135.

58. For an interesting discussion of the liberating dimensions of Christianity with particular reference to Jewish law, see Terrance Callan, *Forgetting the Roots* (New York: Paulist Press, 1986), chap 4.

59. Sebastian Moore, *The Fire and the Rose Are One* (London: Darton, Longman & Todd, 1980), pp. 86–87.

60. Schneiders, p. 46.

61. Ibid.

62. Ibid., pp. 46–47.

Chapter 2/What Matters Is Vision

1. Brennan Manning T.O.R., *The Wisdom of Accepted Tenderness* (Denville, N.J.: Dimension Books, 1978), p. 11.

2. Sandra Schneiders, "Evangelical Equality: Religious Consecration, Mission, and Witness," *Spirituality Today* 39/1 (Spring 1987): 61.

3. Ibid., p. 62.

4. Ibid., pp. 62–63.

5. Ibid., p. 64.

6. Ibid.

7. Ibid., pp. 64–65.

8. Beatrice Bruteau, "Neo-Feminism and the Next Revolution of Consciousness," *Anima* 3/2 (Spring 1977): 11–12.

9. Bernhard Welte, *Meister Eckhart* (Freiburg: Herder, 1979), p. 176.

10. Martin Heidegger, *Die Kehre* (Pfullingen: Günther Neske, 1962), p. 45 (italics and translations with inclusive language mine).

11. Karl Rahner, *The Practice of Faith* (New York: Crossroad, 1983), p. 63 (italics mine).

12. Ibid., p. 63–64 (italics mine).

Chapter 3/Blessed Are the Poor

1. Jim Wallis, *The Call to Conversion* (San Francisco: Harper & Row, 1981), pp. 57–58.

2. Ibid., p. 58.

3. Petru Dumitriu, *To the Unknown God,* trans. James Kirkup (New York: Seabury Press, 1982), pp. 56–57.

4. John Francis Kavanaugh, *Following Christ in a Consumer Society* (Maryknoll, N.Y.: Orbis Books, 1981), p. 26.

5. Wallis, p. 64.

6. Dumitriu, p. 35.

7. Donald Nicholl, *Holiness* (New York: Seabury Press, 1981), p. 21 (italics mine).

8. Ibid., p. 14.

9. Ibid., p. 16.

10. Ibid., p. 18 (italics mine).

11. Ibid., p. 17.

12. Barbara Fiand, *Releasement* (New York: Crossroad, 1987), p. 15.

13. Ibid., pp. 22–27.

14. Ibid., p. 26.

15. Nicholl, pp. 42, 43, 44.

16. Ann Belford Ulanov, *Picturing God* (Cambridge, Mass.: Cowley Publications, 1986), p. 15.

17. Ibid.

18. Ibid., pp. 17–18.

19. Ibid., p. 18.

20. Edward C. Whitmont, *The Symbolic Quest* (Princeton, N.J.: Princeton University Press, 1978), pp. 221–22.

21. Sandra Schneiders, *New Wineskins* (New York: Paulist Press, 1986), p. 181.

22. Ibid.

23. Martin Heidegger, *Discourse on Thinking*, trans. John M. Anderson and E. Hans Freund (New York: Harper Torchbook, 1969), p. 54.

24. Hendrik M. Ruitenbeek, *The Male Myth* (New York: Dell, 1966), pp. 17.

25. Schneiders, p. 91.

Chapter 4/Community for Mission

1. With Sandra Schneiders I agree that "celibacy is the determining characteristic of religious life in a way that neither poverty nor obedience can be. Celibacy distinguishes religious life from other forms of Christian life just as taking another person for one's lawful wedded spouse for better or worse distinguishes marriage from other states of life" (*New Wineskins* [New York: Paulist, 1986], p. 69). Whereas all Christians are asked to follow the will of God in their lives (obedience) and to embrace poverty of spirit—to share with others and be in solidarity with those less fortunate (poverty)—though the way this is done will be different according to one's calling, the vocation to live consecrated celibacy is given only to some and identifies them, therefore, as

of a specific life-orientation. This is what I mean by "celibate identity." (See Schneiders also, p. 114).

2. Mary Wolff-Salin, *The Shadow Side of Community and the Growth of the Self* (New York: Crossroad, 1988), p. 78.

3. Ibid.

4. Ibid.

5. The comparison with marital community is developed well by Mary Wolff-Salin in ibid., p. 23.

6. Ibid., p. 25.

7. Ibid., p. 23.

8. Schneiders, p. 247.

9. Ibid. (italics mine).

10. Joan Chittister (Sr.), *Women, Ministry, and the Church* (New York: Paulist Press, 1983), pp. 32–33 (italics mine).

11. Wolff-Salin, p. 8.

12. A modern example of this can be found in Sr. Joyce Ridick's *Treasures in Earthen Vessels* (New York: Alba House, 1984), chap. 2.

13. Karl Rahner, *The Practice of Faith* (New York: Crossroad, 1983), p. 62.

14. John Francis Kavanaugh, *Following Christ in a Consumer Society* (Maryknoll, N.Y.: Orbis Books, 1981), p. 38.

15. Barbara Fiand, *Living Religious Vows in an Age of Change* (Cincinnati: St. Anthony Messenger Press, 1989), tape 3.

16. See the section "The Primacy of Disposition" in chap. 2.

17. Rahner, p. 63.

18. See the section "Refounding Our Myths" in chap. 1.

19. See the section "Thinking into Our Myths" in chap. 1.

20. Bernard J. Boelen, *Personal Maturity* (New York: Seabury Press, 1978), pp. x, 12, 128, 129.

21. See the section "Toward a Holistic Paradigm" in chap. 1.

22. See the section "Called to Self-Sacrifice" in chap. 3.

23. Henri J. M. Nouwen, *Clowning in Rome* (Garden City, N.Y.: Image Books, 1979), pp. 37–58.

24. Sebastian Moore, *The Crucified Is No Stranger* (London: Darton, Longman & Todd, 1977); the entire book is a reflection on this theme.

25. See chap. 2, note 12.

26. C. G. Jung, *Psychological Reflections,* selected and edited by Jolande Jacobi and R. F. C. Hull (Princeton, N.J.: Princeton University Press, 1978), p. 365.

27. Kathryn North, "Creative Solitude," *Desert Call: Spiritual Life Institute* 21/3 (Fall 1986): 22.

28. Ibid. (italics mine).

29. Ibid.
30. See the section "A Personal Yes" in chap. 3.
31. Wolff-Salin, p. 25.
32. Jung, pp. 224–25.
33. Ibid.
34. Wolff-Salin, p. 37.
35. Ibid., pp. 37–38 (italics mine).
36. Henri J. M. Nouwen, *Lifesigns* (Garden City, N.Y.: Image Books, 1986), p. 31.
37. Ibid., pp. 31–32.
38. Sebastian Moore, *Inner Loneliness* (New York: Crossroad, 1982), pp. 15–16.
39. Ibid., p. 22.
40. Ibid., p. 34.
41. Cited by Marilyn Wussler S.S.N.D., M.S., "Don't Is a Four Letter Word," *Human Development* 10/1 (Spring 1989): 19.
42. Alice Miller, *Prisoners of Childhood,* trans. Ruth Ward (New York: Basic Books, 1981), p. 15.
43. L. Patrick Carroll, S.J., and Katherine Marie Dyckman, S.N.J.M., *Chaos or Creation* (New York: Paulist Press, 1986), p. 122.
44. Ibid., p. 127.
45. Gerald G. May, M.D., *Will and Spirit* (San Francisco: Harper & Row, 1982), pp. 185–86 (italics mine).
46. As cited by Rick Fields, "Celibacy and Religious Passion," *The Sun* 157 (December 1989): 7 (first set of italics mine).
47. Ibid.
48. Kavanaugh, p. 134.
49. Ibid.
50. Nouwen, *Clowning in Rome,* p. 38.
51. Ibid., p. 52.
52. See note 1, in this chapter, concerning celibacy as the determining characteristic of religious life.

Chapter 5/Creative Fidelity

1. Carolyn McDade, "Song to Mary," *Rain Upon Dry Land* (Plainville, Mass.: Surtsey Publishing, 1984), stanza 6.
2. Ann Belford Ulanov, *Receiving Woman* (Philadelphia: Westminster Press, 1981), pp. 35–36; quoted in Barbara Fiand, *Releasement* (New York: Crossroad, 1987), p. 68.
3. Quoted by Dorothee Soelle, *Beyond Mere Obedience,* trans. Lawrence W. Denef (New York: Pilgrim Press, 1982), p. 8.
4. Ibid.

5. See chap. 1, "Culture in Crisis."

6. Sandra Schneiders, "Evangelical Equality: Religious Consecration, Mission, and Witness," *Spirituality Today* 39/1 (Spring 1987): 60.

7. See the section "Culture in Crisis" in chap. 1.

8. Soelle, chaps. 2, 3, 4.

9. Ibid., p. 7 (italics mine).

10. Ibid., pp. 7–8 (italics mine).

11. Ibid., p. 8.

12. Ibid., pp. 8–9.

13. Stanley Milgram, "A Behavioral Study of Obedience," in *The Norton Reader,* ed. Arthur M. Eastman, 3rd ed. (New York: W. W. Norton & Co., 1973), pp. 293–307. This study documents "a procedure for the study of destructive obedience in the laboratory. It consists of ordering a naive S [subject] to administer increasingly more severe punishment to a victim in the context of a learning experiment. Punishment is administered by means of a shock generator with 30 graded switches ranging from Slight Shock to Danger: Severe Shock. The victim is a confederate of the E [experimenter]. The primary dependent variable is the maximum shock the S is willing to administer before he [she] refuses to continue further. 26 Ss obeyed the experimental commands fully, and administered the highest shock on the generator. 14 Ss broke off the experiment at some point after the victim protested and refused to provide further answers. The procedure created extreme levels of nervous tension in some Ss. Profuse sweating, trembling, and stuttering were typical expressions of this emotional disturbance. One unexpected sign of tension—yet to be explained—was the regular occurrence of nervous laughter, which in some Ss developed into uncontrollable seizures. The variety of interesting behavioral dynamics observed in the experiment, the reality of the situation for the S, . . . point to the fruitfulness of further study."

14. Soelle, p. 9.

15. Ibid., p. 10.

16. Ibid., pp. xiii–xvi.

17. Jim Wallis, *The Call to Conversion* (San Francisco: Harper & Row, 1981), pp. 31–32.

18. Joann Wolski Conn, ed., *Women's Spirituality Resources for Christian Development* (New York: Paulist Press, 1986), p. 11 (italics mine).

19. See the section "No Longer Set Apart" in chap. 2.

20. Sandra Schneiders, *New Wineskins* (New York: Paulist Press, 1986), p. 140 (italics mine).

21. Brennan Manning T.O.R., *The Wisdom of Accepted Tenderness* (Denville, N.J.: Dimension Books, 1986), p. 19.

22. Ibid.

23. Soelle, p. 19.

24. Ibid., pp. 19–20.

25. Ibid., p. 20.

26. Wolski Conn, p. 26. Referring to the ideas of Phyllis Tribble, Conn suggests that "subordination is the consequence of sin; the curse is upon the serpent, not the woman, in Gen. 3." The serpent, of course, is possible in each of us when we are scattered from our inner center.

27. Fyodor Dostoyevsky, *The Brothers Karamazov* (New York: Airmont Publishing, 1966), book 5, chap. 5, pp. 223–39.

28. Ibid., p. 230.

29. Ibid., pp. 230–31.

30. Nicholas Berdyaev, *Dostoyevsky* (Cleveland: World Publishing Co., 1962), p. 70.

31. Soelle, pp. 23–24.

32. I refer the reader back to the discussion of the holistic approach to the meaning of redemption, in the section "Toward a Holistic Paradigm" in chap. 1.

33. Soelle, p. 24.

34. Ibid., p. 26 (italics mine).

35. Fiand, p. 50.

36. Ibid.

37. See the section "Called to Self-Sacrifice" in chap 3. The quote is from Donald Nicholl, *Holiness* (New York: Seabury Press, 1981), p. 21.

38. See the sections "Taking Ownership of Our Feelings," "Living the Tension," and "Our Homesickness for God" in chap. 4.

39. Schneiders, *New Wineskins,* p. 162.

40. Ibid., p. 161.

41. Ibid., p. 164.

42. Kieran Kavanaugh, O.C.D., and Otillio Rodriguez, O.C.D., trans., *The Collected Works of St. John of the Cross* (Washington D.C.: ICS Publications, 1973), p. 714.

43. William Johnson, *Christian Zen* (New York: Harper & Row, 1971), p. 37.

44. Ibid.

45. A plethora of literature has in the last decade or so dealt with these various experiences. For a clear and concise handling of mid-life, its phenomena and its crisis, I refer the reader to Janice Brewi and Ann Brennan, *Celebrate Mid-Life* (New York: Crossroad, 1988).

46. See the section "Our Homesickness for God" in chap. 4.

47. Gerald G. May, M.D., *Will and Spirit* (San Francisco: Harper & Row, 1982), p. 172.

48. Lao Tsu, *Tao Te Ching,* trans. Gia-Fu Feng and Jane English (New York: Vintage Books, 1972), 10 (italics mine).

49. Bernard J. Boelen, *Personal Maturity* (New York: Seabury Press, 1978), p. 158.

50. Ibid., p. 159.

51. Fiand, p. 48.

Chapter 6/Conversion toward Increase

1. Joseph Campbell, *Myths to Live By* (New York: Bantam Books, 1973), p. 13.

2. Ibid.

3. John Shea, *Stories of God* (Chicago: Thomas More Press, 1978), p. 8.

4. Ibid., pp. 7–8 (italics mine).

5. The author of this story is Francis Dorff. It has been cited recently in a number of works: M. Scott Peck cites it in the Prologue of *The Different Drum* (New York: Simon & Schuster, 1988), pp. 13–15; Mary Wolff-Salin, in her book *The Shadow Side of Community and the Growth of the Self* (New York: Crossroad, 1988), pp. 82–83. She claims to have "heard" the story from Joan Chittister, O.S.B., *Living the Rule Today: A Series of Conferences on the Rule of Benedict* (Erie, Penn.: Benet Press, 1982), pp. 98–99.

6. Pierre Teilhard de Chardin, *The Divine Milieu* (New York: Harper & Row), p. 61, quoted here from Shea, p. 45.

7. Ibid.

8. Interview with Donna J. Markham O.P., Ph.D., "The Decline of Vocations in the United States," *New Catholic World* 231/1381 (January/February 1988): 15.

9. Dr. Jackie Schwartz, *Letting Go of Stress* (New York: Pinnacle Books, 1982), pp. 95–97.

10. Ibid., p. 98.

11. Hans Selye, M.D., *The Stress of Life* (New York: McGraw-Hill, 1978), pp. 174–77.

12. Richard A. Stein, M.D., *Personal Strategies for Living With Less Stress* (New York: John Gallagher Communications, 1983), p. 3.

Epilogue

1. Karl Rahner, *The Practice of Faith* (New York: Crossroad, 1983), p. 63 (italics mine).